THE ENERGETICS OF BEHAVIOR

CHANGE YOUR VIBE, SEE YOUR KIDS THRIVE

The *Heart, Mind & Science* Behind Transformative Adult-Child Interactions

MARY ROBINSON REYNOLDS

EnergeticsOfBehavior.com
Heart Productions & Publishing, LLC
Salem, OR 97305

"A leader takes people where they want to go.
A great leader takes people where
they don't necessarily want to go,
but ought to be."
— Eleanor Roosevelt

"Good leaders inspire people to have
confidence in their leader.
Great leaders inspire people to have
confidence in themselves."
— Eleanor Roosevelt

Dedication

*This book is dedicated to
my amazing husband
who believed in the
importance of my message
from the day he asked
for my phone number.*

TABLE OF CONTENTS

WHAT OTHER PEOPLE ARE SAYING

Chantal Snellgrove, Founder of *Parenting Special Needs Magazine* writes ...

"You had me *at Change Your Vibe; See Your Kid Thrive*! I've been going to therapy with my neurodivergent daughter for years, and when I watched your energetics resource video, it was like the light went on at long last—not just about my daughter, but mostly for me.

"The importance of checking in with my energy first and then leaning in to find out what my daughter's take—thoughts and feelings—on the situation is turns things around faster than I ever imagined.

"So often it feels like we're not making a significant difference, and you answered that in the book by saying, 'Remember always that you receive the instant you give and, in that, you can trust you've made a difference in someone's life because you felt it in your own, which gives me the boost I need to keep on keeping on."

Kelly Harris, a PTA Parent said it best …

"I just watched your energetics video that highlights the main concepts in your book.

"Wow! I had so many light bulb moments as I was watching it.

"I am a 45-year-old mom of two girls.

"My oldest daughter is 16, and I can see where I have not been connecting with her and can hardly wait for her to come home from her band camp to start connecting.

"My baby is just 18 months old, and I can see where I have already started the same sad way of reacting to things.

"But now I am certain I can change that too.

"It would be my wish that my school's administration would provide your book for every single person on the faculty and staff. Thank You!"

Kathy Hess-Reneau, Educational Consultant – TX writes …

"Viewing your video from your book brought tears to my eyes.

"Our Superintendent believes in educating the whole child and has been a very innovative leader since she arrived. Each year, she assigns reading material to leadership that is designed to clearly set the tone for positive change.

"I was very impressed with the critical elements you captured in your webinar about energetics to specifically assist teachers and parents in succeeding with ALL children, regardless of the situation.

I wish every person entering the teaching profession were able to read it and discuss it!

"It's a book for ALL people. Wonderful bit of writing. I repeat! I shall read it again many times. Bless you for changing the lives of so many kids."

Doris Wiens, Retired Educator – NE writes ...

"Your latest energetics book and the masterclass are absolute treasures! I wish every teacher and parent would be able to spend two days with you!

"Together, they form a boot camp for teachers and parents. The information is incredibly useful and easily applicable. I repeat! A big 'thank you' for such a healing way to 'think' about behaviors and how best to interrupt them at a thought level.

"I especially enjoyed the relabeling exercise. I shall continue to apply your 'thinking' techniques with my grandchildren and the volunteering I still do in the classroom."

HOW TO USE THIS BOOK

From Theory to Practice:
Making Energetics Work for You with Ease

Let's set our sights on the bigger picture!

I'm so glad you're here! As you begin this journey with me, I want to share something truly special. This isn't just a book; it's an invitation to embark on a transformative journey. Connect your heart and mind with the incredible world of quantum science and innovative energy hacks. These tools will help you fine-tune and fast-track your energetic connections with the children in your life.

I've poured my heart into organizing this book in a way that feels natural and supportive. Each section builds on the last, guiding you through the intuitive and often subtle nuances of energetics. My hope is that you'll find it easier to shift your energy and recognize the amazing transformations in the youth within your biofield of influence.

But first, let's explore what the biofield is. It refers to the energetic field—often shaped like a torus—surrounding and interacting with our bodies. This field significantly influences our physical, emotional, and mental well-being, as well as that of the children around us. Consequently, it paves the way for profound shifts in relationships and mutual understanding.

I break down this journey into three distinct parts:

Part I: VIBES DON'T LIE

In this foundational section, we delve into user-friendly examples of quantum field theory to illuminate the concept of quantum interconnectedness. Here, we unveil how energy flows and co-mingles between you and the children in your life.

The core principle is elegantly simple: your vibes impact your children's behaviors in ways you may not even yet realize.

Have you ever noticed how children act as barometers, reflecting the emotional atmosphere surrounding them? They serve as mirrors, offering insights into aspects of ourselves that may need our attention. Understanding how energy is in play in these dynamics is not just fascinating; it's crucial for fostering healthy and supportive relationships.

Part II: CHANGE YOUR VIBE

Now that you're grounded in the understanding that vibes don't lie, it's time to take action! In this section, I will introduce energy hacking and share true stories that illustrate how even the smallest vibes can undermine even the best intentions.

The exciting part of all of this is that you will see just how quick and easy it can be to turn around the situations that frustrate you the most.

Whether these opportunities involve covert behaviors simmering beneath the surface or overt explosions of energetically laced emotion, you'll find great relief in getting to the heart of the problem and creating productive change.

Part III: SEE YOUR KIDS THRIVE

In this final section, we shine the light on the profound vibrational impact of meaning, labels, and perceptions. The lens through which we view each child directly affects the results we get—a concept scientifically grounded in the self-fulfilling prophecy known as *The Pygmalion Effect.*

If we're not getting the results we desire, it's time to look in the mirror.

I'll guide you through the process of fine-tuning what's not working in your interactions. By shifting our perceptions, expectations, and energy, we can create a welcoming environment where our kids truly thrive, promoting their well-being and success.

My Gifts to You

I write as I teach. You'll notice I frequently recommend additional resources throughout this book; it's a natural inclination of mine as someone who has lived it and understands your challenges—to guide you toward further support. Navigating the complexities of being a teacher, parent, or educational leader often feels daunting, especially when your plate is already full.

As a token of my appreciation for your commitment to this journey, I've designed three micro-dose gift resources to supplement your experience.

I believe you'll find them straightforward and practical, embodying the principles of being Firm, Fair, Fearless, Flexible, Focused, Forthright, and FUNctional.

These resources will seamlessly integrate into your busy life without overwhelming you.

Don't wait! Dive into these gift resources right now and keep them handy as we explore the transformative ideas presented throughout this journey together.

Your Power To Influence Now:
MaryReynolds.com/Gifts

Burying the Lead

For forty years, I buried the lead. Why? Because I was concerned about how some people would receive this information.

I've woven Energetics into every book and online program I've ever created, but not until chapter or module four. I wanted people to experience my energy and expertise so they would not be able to dismiss the importance of Energetics.

It's the crucial missing puzzle piece that can truly connect us with the children we're striving to reach and teach.

I was intentional about not being classified as "woo-woo," as I don't fit into that category, and my insights must not be minimized. They represent a vital component that we all need to understand and act upon.

I recognize that some may resist this information because it emphasizes personal accountability and encourages a return to intuition—a path that might feel counterintuitive in a society where many prefer to point fingers, cling to victim mentality, and assign blame.

At this point in my life, it is no longer about convincing anyone of anything. This book is intended for those who genuinely thirst for Energetics. If that resonates with you, I'm here to offer you great relief because what I know for certain is that people who feel better do better.

This is not about reinventing yourself;
this is about fine-tuning and fast-tracking better results.

The Missing Puzzle Piece

For those doing everything possible to help struggling kids—often experiencing frustratingly elusive progress—I've found that the Energetics of any situation is more often than not the missing piece of the puzzle.

Energetics connect all the dots and significantly improves outcomes, accelerating change faster than you may think. I'm genuinely excited and relieved to finally bring this valuable information to the forefront.

My goal is to illuminate the challenges our kids face today and transform them into opportunities. While we're refining our approaches within educational programs and popular parenting literature, there's still work to be done.

When I initially began teaching about Energetics, it was with a desire to help children like me—who were often "bulldozed" by loving, well-meaning adults—believing that forced compliance could prepare them for the harsh realities of life. Unfortunately, the unintended consequences of these "old-school" methods can make the pathway to a healthy, productive adult life feel painfully difficult.

As I began teaching these concepts for continuing education credits, it became clear that I was not just imparting knowledge about Energetics; I was also seeking to promote healing in the adults who care for today's children, reflecting on their childhood experiences.

I Am All About the Vibes!

In a punitive world, we need an approach rooted in energetic connection before forced correction.

I've had decades of witnessing remarkable transformations that occur simply through a shift in our own vibes. This energetic approach emphasizes skill development, collaboration, and emotional resilience.

My objective is to empower you with effortless Energy Hacks, enabling you to fine-tune and harness your energy, transforming concerning situations into valuable opportunities for understanding and growth.

My goal? To equip you with quick hacks demonstrating how seamlessly shifting your own energy can enhance a child's experience and response.

Reflecting on my experience as my parents' "problem child," I gained two essential insights. I identified: 1) what treatment I despised the most from the adults and peers in my life, and 2) what I wish they would have done differently.

Observe Yourself

In my third-year classroom, there were full-length windows on two sides, one to the outside, the other to the corridor. I was keenly aware of my visibility when teachable moments arose with my students. I cultivated the habit of stepping back to observe myself as if someone else were watching in that moment.

Whenever I caught myself going "old-school," I would quickly ask myself,

"How would I love to be treated at a time like this?"

This simple question consistently directed me toward new and effective solutions. And herein lie the answers you seek!

Your Assignment

As an educator committed to finding better ways, I came up with this mental exercise to replace what had been done to me when I faltered as a child. So before going any further, grab a comforting cup of something warm, settle in with paper and pen, and take a moment to reflect. Draw a line down the middle of the page.

Step 1: On the left-hand side, make a list of the hurtful responses and actions you remember receiving from adults, siblings, and peers that were meant to "teach" you a lesson. As you recall each event, notice how it makes you feel.

After you finish, check in with yourself: Rate your energy on a scale of 1 to 10, with 10 being the highest. What's your energy like right now?

Step 2: Now, on the right-hand side, write down how you would have preferred to be treated in each situation.

After completing this, do another check-in. On a scale of 1 to 10, what's your energy level now?

Step 3: Make it your mission to STOP all practices you identified on the left. Instead, rigorously embrace and implement the preferred responses on the right that you would have loved receiving instead.

It's that simple and straightforward. Commit to actively using the responses that align with your vision for compassionate guidance. Here's my position on kind and firm adulting versus bulldozing and helicoptering children to teach them a lesson:

> Never, ever, ever do to a child what you would
> never, ever, ever do to anyone bigger than you!
> -Mary Robinson Reynolds

Be a consultant to the children in your care. You already know it's possible to stop using hurtful tactics to manage kids.

You already know it's possible to embrace compassion, kindness, collaboration, and skill development to guide children toward emotional resilience. In kindness, we find the strength to uplift others—as well as ourselves.

Change Your Vibe, See Your Kids Thrive!

Welcome to my world of energetics! Let's have some fun while doing this! Together, we can evolve the narrative and create positive impacts on the young lives we touch. Let's get started!

SOMETHING'S OFF!

Have you ever had that feeling in a conversation or situation where something's off?

I'm here to tell you that it probably is, and it may or may not have anything to do with you or something you did or didn't do.

But trust me when I say it's better to know than not to know. You will be relieved to learn that I will show you how to confront non-confrontationally with a few fine-tuning "Energy Hacks."

In this book, we'll explore evidence-based science that demonstrates how incoming energy is real and constantly at play, but more importantly, how diffusing the energies that can escalate situations with kids (and adults) isn't as hard or complicated as you might think.

We'll delve into how you are influencing energy, whether you mean to be or not, and how "what you think about comes about," how it translates—in real time—into blowing things up or soothing things down!

We'll talk about how to read the room, to identify incoming attitudinal energies, vibes, and tones occurring in the present moment.

Most importantly, we'll learn how to bring diffusing energy into any situation, rapidly defusing intense, potentially explosive interactions, in 30 seconds or less, more often than not.

You'll gain insights on how to know what you know, feel what you feel, and want what you want in situations that are either starting to go sideways, already imploding, or becoming explosive.

Suppose you're a student or practitioner of Positive Behavioral Interventions and Supports (PBIS), Collaborative and Proactive Solutions (CPS), Emotional Intelligence (EI), Social-Emotional Learning (SEL), Restorative Practices, and various other intentional approaches to teaching and raising kids.

In that case, you'll likely be relieved to discover the essential element that may have been overlooked:

The Energetics of Behavior

Here's the thing. These contemporary programs share a few key aspects that can enhance your understanding and effectiveness:

1. They begin by reassuring you that it's not your fault, fostering a supportive learning environment.

2. Their purpose is to deepen your understanding of behavior, allowing you to change the lens through which you view what's happening.

3. They often provide comprehensive programs that require significant time and effort to learn and implement—core competencies—while you may already be managing a full plate.

However, they may be overlooking a vital aspect:

Energetics

What's the first thing new understanding brings about?

A shift in perception shifts energy and instantaneously improves an individual's nervous system.

That's when the brain can breathe again, getting oxygen and activating the frontal lobe, allowing the mind to think clearly.

Seeing with "new eyes" is when the magic happens!

We are about to start down a path of discovery on tapping into the energy permeating any interaction—both our own energy and that of others—that can help turn around situations with today's youth quickly and peacefully.

Despite our best intentions, it often feels like we're accidentally escalating issues instead of defusing them.

The Energetic Connection

As you read this, you're about to begin a transformative journey that bridges scientific understanding with practical strategies for navigating the complex behaviors of today's youth.

Life can often feel like a whirlwind, especially when you're dedicated to loving, living, and working with young people who exhibit behaviors that seem, at times, to come out of nowhere.

You know the struggle of feeling like you're constantly on edge, bracing for the next outburst or emotional collapse. With a full plate already filled with responsibilities and obstacles, you need effective and simple tools to implement.

Quickly diffusing the energy of explosive and implosive behaviors is where the concept of energetics comes into play.

The idea is to intervene at the *thought level*, addressing the intentions and expectations that shape behaviors—yours and those of the children with whom you interact.

This approach pivots from diving into diagnosing to exploring the underlying energies that drive behavior. It's about recognizing that, *before* reaching for reasoning or disciplinary measures, you have the power to influence the energetic environment.

Something To Think About

Throughout this book, you will discover my user-friendly approach to evidence-based methodologies grounded in the science of quantum interconnectedness. These insights unveil how crucial our attitudes, vibes, and tones are in shaping the behaviors we may experience with others.

Picture a scenario where you can shift the energy of a room filled with tension or anxiety in 30 seconds or less. Imagine intercepting explosive reactions or imploding episodes with simple energy hacks, empowering you to take charge of the situation before resorting to force.

It's important to acknowledge that owning your part of the behavioral equation comes from a place of compassion and understanding. As you read through these pages, you'll find explanations and encouragement to help you let down your defenses.

It has been my life experience that, as both a participant and an observer, I have found:

> In your most vulnerable moments
> you are actually your most powerful.

Harness the power of Energetics to reclaim your influence and effectiveness, creating seamless synergy in communication and collaboration with today's youth.

The principles you learn here will help you proactively engage with the energetically triggered emotional undercurrents that drive behaviors, rather than merely reacting to them in habitual patterns.

Energetics is the cornerstone underlying every interaction alluded to within the methodologies of Social-Emotional Learning (SEL), Emotional Intelligence (EI), and countless other programs.

> You can be saying and doing all the right things
> but if the attitudinal energies of
> all the participants are in conflict,
> communication breaks down, and
> little lasting change is accomplished.

Your journey reading *The Energetics of Behavior* will be one of empowerment. With extensive speaking, writing, and coaching experience in this field, a master's degree in educational psychology, counseling, and development, along with my background in drug, alcohol, and family counseling, I aim to guide you toward mastering this crucial aspect of human interaction at home, in the classroom, and in leading.

So, embrace this invitation to dive into the material you're reading. You have what it takes to change your understanding of behaviors and how you engage with the youth in your life.

Let's begin this exploration together—your adventure towards energetic understanding starts now!

Happy Influencing!

MAKIN' MAGIC

I grew up in a small farming community where elementary, junior high, and high school coexisted under one roof. Despite my struggles with my parents during my senior year in high school, something remarkable started to happen that fall: each morning, as I stepped off the bus, ten to twenty elementary kids would swarm around me, excited to take turns holding my hands as we all walked toward school together.

I wondered why all the children were so excited to greet me. It baffled me, but rather than dwell on it, I decided I just had some special magic that my peers didn't seem to have. I left it at that and cherished those moments of being welcomed into school every morning.

Years later, as my teaching career began, I creatively tapped into that magic in my classroom. I even told my young students that my desk was magical; whenever they approached with questions, I knew that if I waited just a moment—30 seconds or less—they would usually find the answers themselves. We made a game of it! When students felt uncertain about their answers, they'd stroll over to my desk, and together we would wait in anticipation to see what magical insights emerged.

By my third year of teaching, I realized that this magic was about what happens energetically when we remove limiting labels and, therefore, expectations from a child (or anyone, for that matter).

Holding a high vision gives off a vibe that opens up potential and creates waves of encouraging energy.

While it might appear to be magic, it's about shifting perceptions and decisions—turning FEAR: False Evidence Appearing Real (illusion) into empowering outcomes. It's all about the meaning we give an event or outcome.

In other words, it's all about expectation. Expectation, when conveyed with genuine regard, respect, and lightheartedness, can change everything for the better, just like magic!

This kind of magic is about suspending judgment by listening to and acting on our own intuition, being open and receptive to the intuitions of others.

Now, let's fast-forward to my ninth year of teaching when life threw me a series of curve balls.

In 1984, I experienced the devastating loss of my first child at birth, followed by a miscarriage just three months later. A year later, I faced a high-risk pregnancy that resulted in a premature birth. One year after our son was born, I went through a divorce. Shortly thereafter, I relocated to a new state, only to find that job prospects and interviews were falling through. I found myself as a single mother of a two-year-old and completely alone.

   CHANGE YOUR VIBE, SEE YOUR KIDS THRIVE

I was emotionally and physically burned out, literally living on pennies, alone in a vast new city where I knew no one.

My life hurt so bad; it felt like someone was running their fingernails down the chalkboard of my soul.

All my adult life, I had worked so hard to do everything the "right" way.

And now, here I was.

With the precious exception of my wonderful son, I had somehow managed to find myself with everything in life that I did not want!

From Burnout to Breakthrough!

At the height of my burnout, while grappling with how to support myself and my son, I was having lunch with a new professional aquaintance, Connie Dawson, an educational consultant and co-author of *Growing Up Again: Parenting Ourselves, Parenting Our Children*. After listening to my story, she bluntly asked me:

"What's great about you?
What is it that you do best, Mary?"

Without skipping a beat, I said:

"I make magic with the youth who are
at risk of being lost through the cracks of our schools;
the kids being kicked out their classrooms."

To which she replied:

> "Excellent, but I don't think magic will sell itself!
> What is it exactly that you do with students
> that other educators are not doing?"

> "What is the magic?"

For the first time in my life, I felt my purpose coming up through me, filling up the hole in my soul. I immediately rushed home, grabbed some paper and a pen, and my system—the magic—literally wrote itself.

My Makin' Magic booklet came to life! MaryReynolds.com/Gifts

Within three months, I developed my *Breaking the Cycles of Failure: Teacher As Consultant Training (T.A.C.T.)* program and taught it for the first time through the Portland State University—Multnomah Continuing Education division for CEU credit.

This moment began a quest to explain my magic and teach others how to access it, too.

> I wanted to lead my CEU students to understand my "magic" through the scientific lens of the quantum field theory and interconnectedness. I empowered them to understand what's happening energetically and how to use it proactively.

This magic is the same system I've applied to my life, my second marriage, and my blended family for the past four decades. I still love seeing the light turn on in people's eyes as I teach it. Teaching and coaching continue to fill my soul every day.

Teaching *The Energetics of Behavior* as a program is profoundly important to me because I've seen how painful life can be when you feel you've tried so hard, yet it "appears" that you are failing so big with children and adults alike. MaryReynolds.com/MC

It can be incredibly frustrating to have a lesson to teach or a message to share and not know how to create an energetic connection and engagement amid today's noise and distractions.

On the flip side, I've also witnessed how remarkable life can be when you understand how to intentionally use your energy—your attitudes, vibes, and tones—to engage children and adults fully every step of the way.

And that's just the tip of the iceberg.

As I began the healing work of reigniting the light within me, I discovered that life demands that I BE more, not that I expend more.

Life urges us to acquire empowering skills that enable us to navigate every aspect of our lives more effectively, allowing us to step into the success we are inherently designed to achieve.

Now, I'm doing something I never imagined over four decades ago.

I'm helping teachers, parents, educational leaders, school counselors, psychologists, and grandparents with big hearts who want to make an uplifting, healing difference in navigating the concerns they face with today's Opportunity Kids.

I prefer the term "Opportunity" to "challenging," as it relabels how we perceive children. Think about how you'd feel if you were labeled "challenging."

Additionally, I coach adults and adolescents who struggle to communicate effectively with energetically triggering people and situations.

In short, I teach people how to peacefully turn around the big, scary, emotionally intense situations that have become the new normal in today's classrooms, homes, and workplaces, all within 30 seconds or less, more often than not.

As I write this, I am thinking about you and wondering if you feel burned out. Are you struggling to put into words what's de-energizing you most right now?

Does it feel as though everything is overwhelmingly "hard" right now?

I'm here to help you transform that feeling of "hard" into an easier and far more enjoyable experience of loving, living, and working with today's children and other adults.

As we weave together the themes of "Makin' Magic," the profound insights of quantum interconnectedness, and the neurophysiological impact of vibes on the mind and body, we arrive at a compelling understanding: our individual energies and attitudes have the power to transform not only our own experiences but also the lives of those around us.

When swarmed by excited elementary students, the magic I felt as a teenager was not merely whimsical; it stemmed from a genuine energetic connection filled with joy, curiosity, and compassionate acceptance.

This early experience laid the foundation for my exploration into understanding and teaching the role of energy in shaping behavior.

Through my training and personal experiences, I discovered that having a high vision for others—removing limiting labels and nurturing an atmosphere of trust and respect—creates a ripple effect.

Having this knowledge enhances energetically soothing engagement, emotional regulation, and psychological well-being.

Delving into quantum interconnectedness reinforces this understanding.

Our vibes, rooted in our intentions and emotional states, have a direct neurophysiological impact on ourselves and those around us.

Research continues to illustrate how non-judgmental interactions can reduce stress, improve mental clarity, and foster resilience, underscoring the critical role of energy in behavior and learning.

> Just as particles in the quantum field exist
> in an intricate web of interrelation,
> similarly our thoughts, vibrations,
> and energies form a vast network
> of influence, shaping our experiences
> with the youth we aim to support.

In essence, the "magic" we bring into our interactions aligns with the scientific principles governing energy exchanges within each of our circles of influence.

When we nurture a culture of empathy and optimistic expectation, we elevate the collective consciousness, lifting not only ourselves but also the young minds we guide toward a brighter future.

As we continue on this journey of understanding the energetics of behavior, let us remain mindful of the profound interconnected-ness that exists among us.

By consciously harnessing our energies and cultivating environ-ments that transmit peaceful vibes, we unlock a deeper potential within ourselves and those we aim to uplift, influence, and inspire.

Together, we can transform our classrooms, homes, and communi-ties into spaces where today's children thrive not just as an abstract idea but as a tangible reality—one rooted in love, support, and the limitless possibilities that arise when we recognize our individual potential and our shared humanity.

PART I:
VIBES DON'T LIE

It's real, it's happening
whether you mean
for it to be or not!

It's the elephant
in every room and every
intimate conversation!

We're either
blowing things up or
soothing things down.

CHAPTER 1

WHAT IS ENERGETICS?

Working with teachers, parents, coaches, counselors, and educational leaders for over forty years, I have found that *The Energetics of Behavior* is often the missing puzzle piece on the road to a phenomenally joyous experience with today's children.

We will explore energetics, quantum physics, and neuroscientific research to help us all better navigate adult-child relationships in the ways that best prepare children for a life well lived.

I love teaching how to use your energy, rather than physical or emotional force, to turn around problematic situations with the children you love, live with, and work alongside.

You see, we're not just healing today's children; it begins with healing ourselves.

Every relationship is a two-way street, and the faster we embrace the fact that we actually have the power to energetically influence others, the happier our life experiences will be.

I have primarily focused my research and understanding on the science of quantum mechanics and interconnectedness.

My methods and teaching are based on a fundamental principle, which I describe as:

> Energetics is the frequency of our inner state
> that others can see, feel, hear, and sense
> as our attitudes, vibes, and tones.
> -Mary Robinson Reynolds

Now, to truly grasp the transformative power of energetics, consider how smartphones have changed our lives. Before they changed the game, we navigated communication through a maze of devices and channels.

This is similar to how our understanding of behavior has often been scattered across traditional frameworks like PBIS (Positive Behavioral Interventions and Supports), ABA (Applied Behavioral Analysis), and PBS (Positive Behavior Support). These methods prioritize external behaviors but frequently overlook the internal energy dynamics that underpin all relationships.

> Just as smartphones have streamlined how we
> communicate, we can transform
> how we perceive and address behavior.

After smartphones became integral to our lives, everything changed. We gained immediate access to communication, information, and connection in a seamless way, allowing us to navigate our relationships and interactions with greater ease, speed, and effectiveness.

Similarly, after learning about energetics, we begin to see the invisible frequencies that influence our interactions and relationships.

Just as we now can't imagine life without smartphones, once you learn about energetics, you will find it impossible to not know—to "un-know"—how deeply these energies impact every conversation, reaction, and action you take.

Much like smartphones' comfort and convenience, understanding energy dynamics enables us to transform intensely uncomfortable interactions into connections filled with the empowering uplifting vibes of curiosity, compassion, and understanding.

While smartphones consolidate communication, awareness of energetics quickens our understanding of ourselves and our impact on others, revealing the effects of the attitudes, vibes, and tones that permeate every relationship.

One effective energy hack I use often is an AFZ, or Attitude Free Zone. An AFZ is a mental space where I consciously suspend judgment and remain open to understanding others' perspectives. This creates a "safe space" for others, allowing for more constructive dialogue.

As we learn how to view our world through this new lens, we can see that, just as smartphones have reshaped our day-to-day lives, learning about energetics can revolutionize how we engage with the children we love and the environments in which we work.

By harnessing the power of our energy, we can catalyze positive change that creates a ripple effect, enriching our lives and the lives of those around us.

As I always like to say:

> You Can't Have an Attitude and Keep It A Secret!
> -Mary Robinson Reynolds

The term "attitudinal energy" describes the profound impact our inner state has on our surroundings.

Now, let's talk energetics—the transformative principle you didn't know you needed but won't be able to forget once we explore it together. Think of it as the next essential tool in your growth tool-kit, like the microwave or smartphone—once you understand what it can do for you, you'll wonder how you lived without it!

That's what learning about the energetics of behavior will do for you.

Once you grasp how real this is, you will not be able to live a day without it being at the forefront of your awareness in every conversation, reaction, and action you take from this day forward.

> Energetics—attitudes, vibes and tones—
> are the elephant in every room.

It's the thing everybody intuitively knows. We're all picking up on the attitudes, vibes, and tones, but we've never figured out how to talk about what we are sensing without getting megaphone blow-back, until now!

The first factor with energy is that we don't get a computer readout because it is invisible. Not having this computer readout is actually a good thing; if we were aware of everything others think—or don't think—about us all day, it would drive us crazy.

The second factor with energy is that as soon as you label it by calling it a contagion, bad, narcissistic, toxic, or labeling someone as an energy vampire, you get more of it from the very people you want less of. The result of the ensuing conversation is that you are the one who is de-energized. Not them.

If you decide to grow thick skin and build an envisioned shield or wall of protection around yourself, you may also inadvertently wall yourself off from all the good vibes in the world.

This is a critical realization: you are de-energizing yourself, not the people you attribute it to!

Why is that?

As you will see, you are the one judging others and investing your thoughts and, therefore, your energy into them.

They don't care, so they don't expend energy unless or until they pick up on your energy and decide to push back, fight back, or judge back. When this happens, the entire atmosphere feels off until one of you gets to a place of peace.

The process of recognizing how thoughts and energy instantly influence interactions with others is what we will be exploring together throughout this book.

The concept of energy exchange supports the idea that when you invest emotional energy into your perceptions of others, you create an atmosphere that can be significantly influenced by those judgments.

This energy is palpable. The moment someone picks up on it—whether to resist or mirror your energy, vibes, and tones—the overall dynamic shifts, and suddenly, tension fills the air and stays there until one person returns to peace.

Recognizing how your thoughts and energy influence your interactions with others is essential for building happy, healthy relationships.

Every conversation you engage in has the potential for positive or negative energy.

When you bring judgment into the mix, you invite volatility. It's crucial to be aware of how the energy of your thoughts and emotions affects your interactions!

If you want to maintain harmonious relationships, focus on cultivating peaceful, non-judgmental energy.

For instance, I've seen firsthand how a slight shift in my energy can completely transform a tough conversation into a productive dialogue.

Instead of meeting resistance with more judgment, I choose to suspend all judgment for the moment and maintain an AFZ: Attitude Free Zone, until I know more about what's actually going on.

As I demonstrate in my *Miracle Regulator* Micro-Dose resource videos, peaceful thoughts can diffuse the situation and often lead to deeper connections and solutions that benefit everyone involved.

Transformation can happen in as little as 30 seconds or less, more often than not by remembering to do just ONE thing. If you're ready to learn about my discovery check it out at:

MiracleRegulator.com

In it, I delve deeper into the incredible impact of personal energy in diffusing your own or others' attitude and behaviors. By learning to think just ONE thing, you can create a more synergistic environment for yourself and those around you, instantly.

You're Not Alone: Understanding the Real Impact of Your Energy

If you've been struggling with this, let me assure you that you are not the only one.

I have spoken on *Powerful Communication Skills* to over twenty thousand people across the United States in a two-year period. I was evaluated every day, and the #1 comment people would give me after a speaking or training event is:

> "Thank God for your training today, Mary,
> now I know I'm not crazy!"

So, let me reiterate this firmly: you are not crazy!

The energy of how you may be inadvertently connecting with your attitudes, vibes, and tones is real. It's permeating and happening right smack dab in the middle of every interaction you have.

Whether you mean for it to be happening or not, it's all about the attitudes, vibes, and tones.

You may be thinking. "Sounds like a bunch of woo-woo to me."

And that's precisely why I'm here to take the woo out of woo-woo with my user-friendly explanations of replicable, evidence-based science.

So, what exactly is this "replicable, evidence-based science?" It's not just some abstract concept. It's Quantum physics.

To summarize Einstein's Theory of Relativity in three words:

> Everything Is Energy!

David Bohm, the renowned physicist, conceived of solid matter as a hologram-like interference pattern of energy waves. He theorized that human consciousness receives these waves like a radio antenna.

There is a heated debate about it, but it is clear that much more is happening in the unseen realm of human communication than can be explained.

So, what have we learned up to this point?

As we have explored, the energy of your attitudes, vibes, and tones is not just a passing notion; it is a foundational element that influences every interaction in your life.

Understanding that this energy is real and impactful begins to clarify how we connect with one another.

What's coming?

In the next chapter, we will delve deeper into the energetics of behavior itself, examining the principles that govern how our inner states influence not only our experiences but also the dynamics of our relationships with others.

We will explore key concepts from quantum physics that further illuminate how we can harness this knowledge to create more constructive and meaningful interactions.

Get ready to discover how your understanding of energetics can empower you to navigate your relationships more easily and transformatively.

Let's improve our interactions together!

CHAPTER 2

WHAT IS THE ENERGETICS OF BEHAVIOR?

To answer the question, "How do energetics impact behavior?" we must understand that every thought has its own vibrational frequency or wave frequency. These frequencies fuel emotions within us and influence those around us.

> Children are like little sponges, absorbing
> incoming vibes either directly or indirectly
> from the adults and peers in the room,
> often feeling overwhelmed and reactive.
>
> -Mary Robinson Reynolds

Misguided thoughts—life-limiting labels, diagnoses, judgments, and biases—are transmitted through our attitudes, vibes, and tones, triggering uncomfortable feelings in those we have connections with.

These feelings can fuel problematic behavior if we don't help children identify what's concerning them—what's coming at them energetically that they are picking up on—and diffuse it through relabeling and compassionate curiosity.

Now, let's dive deeper.

Have you ever considered what a thought actually is?

In essence, a thought is an energy pattern in the brain. Thanks to modern neuroscience, we can measure these patterns as electro-magnetic activity, commonly known as brainwaves.

Thoughts are invisible, yet they transmit energy, frequencies, and vibrations in the middle of every conversation and non-verbal interaction.

The energy of our thoughts is broadcast to the quantum field and, as Einstein put it:

> "What happens in one part of the quantum field
> influences what happens in another part
> of the field in the same instant."

He called this proven fact "spooky action at a distance."

Our thoughts are not merely personal; they resonate across distances, weaving a tapestry of influence that spans the globe. Each thought matters in the grand scheme of the universe, creating ripples that can uplift or diminish.

Quantum Interconnectedness isn't just theory; it's a crucial under-standing of our energetic impact on each other.

Why is this so important?

As you will see in Experiments #1, #2, and #3, thoughts have vibrational frequencies, they are transmitted as energy that we all pick up on, are infused by, and react to.

Vibes Don't Lie!

Children, in particular, are receptive to these frequencies because their brains are still developing and have fewer distracting concerns and stresses than most adults. So, when a child suddenly blows up or shuts down, something is happening beneath the surface, whether you can see it or not.

As we delve into energetics, you'll discover simple methods for recognizing nonverbal cues and the energetic shifts that occur around us.

Here's the exciting part: by focusing on these energetic factors first, you'll avoid the overwhelm of memorizing endless lists and phrases that can escape you in a moment of escalated emotions.

Instead, I'm excited to demonstrate how straightforward and transformative the process of energy hacking can be, empowering you to harness these tools in your life today!

We've all heard that words can hurt—consider, for instance, the long-lasting impact of calling a child a "brat." Words resonate at specific vibrational frequencies, and the emotions they trigger greatly affect how they are received by others.

However, unspoken words—the internalized beliefs that manifest as thoughts—can often be even more problematic and damaging, because they occur far more frequently and persistently than a few words. And thoughts emerge as energy vibrations which are felt by others.

The solutions you seek to resolve the problematic behaviors keeping you up at night can be as simple as hacking into the underlying energy dynamics, not just for yourself but also for the child.

That's right!

The goal is to deliberately influence better outcomes in how you can connect vibrationally. *Energetics of Behavior* is a powerful tool that can shift the dynamics in your classroom, family atmosphere, and even your work culture.

When you understand how quickly you can turn the energy of a situation around, you can feel more confident about managing your environment effectively. Learning how to intercede energetically will actually win back time for you throughout each day. It's cumulative, and it can reignite your life.

Now I know what you're thinking.

"No one can Vulcan mind-meld a kid into good behavior."

You've read books, searched online, consulted specialists, attended regular IEP or 504 meetings, and used rewards, punishments and contracts for problematic behaviors.

You've been doing the HAALTS method check-in to evaluate if they are Hungry, Angry, Anxious, Lonely, Tired, or spending too much time on Screens when you notice a child getting increasingly irritated.

You understand the Iceberg Theory for looking beneath the surface, but even with these tools, you might still struggle with certain children.

Here's the thing: you could be using some of the best strategies available, but I assert that 80% of successful behavior management comes from Energetics, while 20% is based on strategy.

In light of Einstein's theory, could it even be argued that it's 100% Energetics and 0% strategy? This might be the case, as even the most effective strategy can fall flat if it's undermined by a condescending attitude, judgmental vibe, eye-roll, or harsh tone.

The way to intercede on detrimental
incoming attitudes, vibes, and tones
may not be what you think it will be.

If you can't leave a room or escape a judgmental person, particularly in situations children face daily, you will be well served by learning how to transform that adverse energy, moment by moment with *Miracle Regulator* Micro-Dose resource videos at: MiracleRegulator.com

We're diving into energy—no more running from it, growing thick skin, or shielding ourselves with hypothetical protective walls.

Instead, I intend to share in Part II, three of my easiest-to-remember energy hacks that can turn around problematic behaviors and situations, in 30 seconds or less more often than not, with outstanding results.

Contrary to traditional schools of thought and teaching, behavior management isn't about using force or masterfully applying a multitude of strategies, tools, scripts, tips, and techniques. However, you are welcome to utilize those methods if you still find them necessary after you learn how to use your energy to influence problematic behavior.

What I have to show you will not be pages and pages of scripts and phrases that you will never remember in the heat of the moment.

It's all about the energy of connection.

Yours.

The adult in the room.

Something To Think About

As we conclude this chapter, I hope you recognize the profound impact the attitudinal energy we bring to every situation has on our interactions, especially on how we influence the children in our lives.

By tapping into the power of our thoughts and their vibrational frequencies, we unlock transformative change, creating environments where problematic behaviors dissipate.

Understanding these energetic dynamics equips us to teach children the necessary intuitive based social-emotional skills for navigating their emotions and connections with others.

Now, let's explore the concept of quantum interconnectedness. We'll unpack the replicable, evidence-based science that explains why these energetic influences matter, illuminating how our thoughts and emotions intricately link with the quantum landscape.

I'm excited to explore how these scientific principles apply to your everyday interactions and gain actionable insights that empower you to foster deeper relationships and vibrant connections.

Together, we'll create an environment in which behavior improves not through sheer effort but through energetic alignment.

CHAPTER 3

EVIDENCE-BASED SCIENCE OF QUANTUM CONNECTIONS

Growing up, I never enjoyed science class, and during my first two years of teaching, I found it to be a struggle. Then I made a pivotal decision: I chose to infuse fun into the subject. And you know what? It worked!

Fast forward to today. I find myself immersed in the fascinating realms of quantum interconnectedness and neurophysics, particularly in relation to co-mingling energies. Life has a funny way of guiding you to places you least expect!

Harnessing Invisible Influences on Behavior

I won't sugarcoat it—quantum field theory isn't exactly my comfort zone. Yet, when I sought to explain the sheer magic I felt in high school, especially when hopping off the bus each morning, I became genuinely intrigued. I wanted to unravel this mystery to articulate precisely what that magic was all about. At times, I felt like the Pied Piper, leading children through the wonders of discovery!

Now, if science isn't your thing, fear not! I'm here to guide you through twelve experiments and insights that reveal the invisible influences at play—clues that we have not previously been taught to recognize, yet which can profoundly impact our lives and the children around us.

Take, for instance, the topic of *The Energetics of Behavior*. You won't find this concept in the DSM-5—the Diagnostic and Statistical Manual of Mental Disorders, Fifth Edition—yet I genuinely believe it should be front and center. It has vital implications when mental health care professionals are diagnosing disorders or trying to make sense of seemingly unexplainable behaviors.

Get ready for a journey—an expedition to articulate the scientific basis of what you've felt deeply in your heart and gut. You know it to be true, even if you haven't quite put it into words.

You don't need a PhD to grasp the evidence I'm laying out. Why? Because we're about to see how to turn around intense situations that have many adults in anguish over children struggling in school and at home.

The Ripple Effect of Adult Attitudes on Kids

In the following pages, we will delve into the energetics of human interaction. I aim to demonstrate how both the principles of interconnectedness and insights from neuroscience shed light on the significant ways adults' attitudes, energy, tone, expectations, and life-limiting labels affect children.

Every interaction matters and understanding this dynamic can lead to profound implications for personal growth and development. From our facial expressions and body language to the subtle nuances of our behavior, adults play a pivotal role in shaping how children see themselves and the world around them.

Think about it: our energetic and emotional responses shape the very essence of how children view themselves. It's not just the words we say, it's the energy infused within those words that resonates deeply with young minds. I've witnessed this firsthand during my teaching experience. A simple shift in attitude or tone can spark curiosity or extinguish it, nurture a child's confidence or stifle it.

So, let's embrace this responsibility! Armed with insights from science and a commitment to fostering a synergistic environment, we can make deliberate choices to uplift and empower the next generation.

Remember, the vibrational frequencies we emit ripple out to those around us, creating a powerful feedback loop that shapes not only individual interactions but the broader social landscape.

Understanding the energy dynamics at play is crucial, as it underscores the importance of creating empowering environments that nurture children's growth and potential.

Children home in on the vibrational frequencies emitted by the adults and peers around them. Their developing brains are like sponges, soaking up external cues and signals.

When adults transmit acceptance, encouragement, and belief in a child's potential, those uplifting energies resonate, fostering a sense of safety, confidence, and self-worth.

However, when adults harbor negative thoughts, limiting beliefs, or harsh judgments, even when unspoken, those vibrations are palpable—potentially leading children to experience insecurity, anxiety, and diminished self-esteem.

Psychology and neuroscience research backs this up! Kids absorb and react to the emotional atmosphere created by the adults around them, homing in on the subtleties of tone, body language, and even unspoken thoughts.

The result? A child might internalize an adult's concerns or biases, manifesting in behaviors like withdrawal, defiance, or a reluctance to engage in new experiences.

Let's dig deeper.

Children's self-concepts flourish or falter based on how they interpret the attitudes of the significant adults around them.

If a child senses an adult holds a limiting belief about them, perhaps labeling them as "challenging" or "not good at math," they may start embodying that label, stifling their true potential. This phenomenon, known as the "self-fulfilling prophecy," starkly illustrates the power of adult perceptions and their tangible impact on a child's development.

Consider this: the vibrational frequencies of our thoughts about children create a powerful feedback loop. We're shaping their emotional landscapes and influencing their very development.

> As adults, we must cultivate mindful awareness
> of our thoughts and beliefs.

For example, whenever I shifted my attitude in the classroom, as well as at home, I witnessed an immediate improvement in my kids' engagement and confidence.

We must explore how we can make a similar impact as the adult in the room!

Let's recognize that our energetic environment can foster resilience and empowerment or contribute to the myriad struggles children might face.

So, the next time you interact with a child, pause momentarily.

What energy are you transmitting?

Are you nurturing their potential or inadvertently casting a shadow?

Remember, your words, energy, and attitudes ripple through them in ways that can inspire greatness or hinder growth.

Let's create waves of peace and positivity that help our children shine!

The search for truth ...

is like standing at a ten-foot-high, solid wooden fence
It's too long to get around and too high to climb,
so our only option is to find some little knothole in the fence,
poke our eyeball in, and see what we can see.
Now on the other side of the fence is a cow.
Some people look through the hole and see a horn
and they say, "Ah, the horn is the truth."
Others look through and see the beautiful brown skin
and say, "Ah, brown must be truth."
Then others look through and see the tail
swishing back and forth and are convinced
that the ever-moving tail is the way.
While they all see part of the picture,
no one person can see it all.
-Author Unknown

CHAPTER 4

YOU CAN'T HAVE AN ATTITUDE AND KEEP IT A SECRET!

You've heard the saying, "You only get one first impression!"

Let's take this idea to a new level today.

Throughout my years of teaching, I've found that everyone can relate to Attitudinal Energy in one way or another.

#1 Breakdown in Communication: Attitudinal Energy

Here's a scenario you might recognize:

Sally is starting a new job and introducing herself around the company.

She greets each person she meets by saying, "Hello. I'm Sally, your new team member, and I'm excited to meet and work with you. And your name is?"

They respond by giving her their name.

They chat for a bit, then pull her aside and whisper, "You'll do well here, but make sure you stay away from Robert, because he is 'bad news' for everyone on our team."

Sally continues to meet and introduce herself to people, and each of the next seven people she meets has something disparaging to say or imply about Robert.

Then she comes up to the eighth person and gets to the part where she says,

"And your name is?" He responds, "My name is Robert."

Now at that moment, an unspoken vibrational message is automatically being sent by Sally, energetically: *Bad News equals Bad Vibes!*

Unless, of course, Sally has read this book, is very aware of what's been going on, and has made a conscious decision to suspend all judgment and remain attitudinally gracious to Robert when she meets him for the first time.

Can you relate to this?

First impressions are instantly energetic. It's a defining moment because, in that split second, we can accept everything we've been told about this person, and he will feel an infinitesimal "negative energy hit" from us the instant he introduces himself.

Or we can "get selective amnesia" by deliberately and intentionally refusing to believe anything about him that we've been told so far.

We can shake his hand and connect with him from an intentional AFZ: Attitude Free Zone, firmly refusing to let any of the previous information in, allowing ourselves to meet the person himself, not

     CHANGE YOUR VIBE, SEE YOUR KIDS THRIVE

the labels we've been given about him. We can simply learn to trust our own intuition and energy with new people.

Now let's consider what others have told us about the children in our classrooms or how our relatives treat each of our children, with or without using their words.

I was once invited to a colleague's family gathering where a young mother and her daughter were visiting. It had been a while since her two sisters, mother, and father had been with her now three-year-old, who looked like she was four, going on eighteen!

Her daughter had very normal age-related behaviors, and as I observed the family's distress with her big emotions, it was easy to read their facial expressions from what they were most likely thinking: brat, spoiled, wild child, difficult, handful, challenging, spirited, complex, etc.

When you learn to watch for energetically-laced nonverbal cues, you'll even start picking up on the ickiness of the resulting vibes. (We've all seen this. The relative at the dinner table who snidely remarks under their breath, "Gentle parenting doesn't work," yet loudly enough for everyone to hear and feel.)

I could not only see the judgment, but I could also feel it, and I was sitting across the room. Even I didn't want to be near them—and I'm an adult!

The young mother came over to where I was sitting and wanted me to know that she didn't want my feelings hurt if her young daughter wouldn't come to me because the girl had already rejected her grandmother and both aunts earlier. She'd refused to let them near her. I could see why, and I wasn't surprised.

I thanked her for thinking of me and told her not to worry. Moments later, to everyone's surprise, her daughter ran over to me, jumped in my lap, and showered me with hugs and kisses. She stayed with me for about twenty minutes.

What is the Magic?

The magic lies in my energy—my biofield—where I consciously suspend judgment, labeling, or fault-finding. I strive to approach behavior with understanding rather than fear. As a result, my energy is often warm, welcoming, and soothing.

It's not hard. It's intentional. I choose to practice using it because it brings me such peace and joy. The energetic impact of what we think, judge, and find fault with is real, and it's happening.

We're all doing it.

Influencing behavior energetically is not about mind control. It's about the fact that we've all contributed to upsets, whether we meant to or not.

It involves a collective contribution to emotional disturbances or conflicts, whether intentional or unintentional.

Everyone participates in these disruptions through judgments, attitudes, and energy projections.

This dynamic unfolds in the present moment, and it can be amplified by accumulated emotions and interactions, unless we are holding an Attitude Free Zone.

The following chapters promise to provide specific insights into how this influence operates.

Energetic influence is, in fact, happening in real-time as well as in built-up judgmental attitudes, vibes, and tones over time, and you will see precisely how.

Simply put, the energetics of behavior arise when unproductive and problematic behavior surfaces due to the energy in the room. This energy can be coming at us directly or indirectly as an adult's—sibling's or peer's—attitudes, vibes, and tones based on what they've decided is the truth about a child or the situation they are experiencing.

By the same token, "incoming" energy via judgment, fault-finding, and biases creates thoughts, creates emotions, creates behavior:

Thoughts create energy,
energy creates emotions,
emotions create behavior.

Do not despair.

The solutions we're building up to are far simpler and more straightforward than you may believe is possible right now.

Energy first, tools second.

Because of this, we're slowing everything down to learn about evidence-based science first, so you won't minimize the importance of the tools you will be learning. Your commitment to practice using energetics daily is the cornerstone to improving every area of your life that is not peaceful, fulfilling, or productive.

Here we go: Energy first, tools second, if you still need them!

CHAPTER 5

THOUGHTS REACH OUT INTO OUR WORLD

In our everyday lives, we often encounter moments that hint at a deeper connection between our thoughts and the world around us. From instinctual feelings to uncanny coincidences, these experiences suggest that our thoughts can reach out, influencing our perceptions and interactions in ways we may not, up until now, fully understand.

Here are some examples of how thoughts reach out into the world:

- How often have you been in public and felt that somebody was looking at you? Then you discovered that, sure enough, somebody was!

- Have you had—out of the blue—a thought about someone, then the phone rings, and it's that person?

- Have you ever met someone you were instantly uncomfortable with for no apparent reason?

- Have you ever sensed that your children were doing something they shouldn't, and you feel an urge to check on them? Sure enough, you find they're about to do something that could cause them harm!

- Do you have a dog who wakes up from her nap, gets off the couch, and goes to the door to wait just before a family member arrives home—but well before she could possibly hear the car? (According to my husband, who can see my location on his phone, our dog gets up and watches the door to the garage as soon as I turn into our neighborhood, and I don't have a consistent schedule.)

Tuning Into the Experience

We think of these things as extraordinary, but in fact, they are very common and available to all of us all the time.

Whether or not we notice and observe these events depends upon whether we can step back from our busy lives and let ourselves tune into and be conscious of what's happening around us.

The information you will receive here may be something you already intuitively know or have felt but couldn't quite put your finger on, or it may be fresh and exciting news. Regardless, this information can free you.

On the other hand, this information may be frightening and disconcerting. It suggests that we are, at the very least, genuinely empowered. In fact, we are utilizing this power every moment of every day, whether we recognize it or not, and whether we intend to or not.

In order for your attitude to be the most powerful influencing agent working for you, you must continuously be willing to explore the power you generate inside yourself by what you think, believe and, therefore, transmit to others.

Our thoughts are more than mere reflections; they are powerful currents that shape our reality and influence everyone around us. Every idea, every belief, every fleeting emotion sends out waves of energy that can affect not only our experiences but also the people and environments we engage with.

Recognizing this dynamic interplay reminds us of our profound interconnectedness, providing us with an opportunity to recognize the power we hold over our realities through our mindset.

By tapping into this potential, we have the opportunity to turn our lives into a canvas of possibilities, actively shaping our relationships and experiences in ways we may have never considered. Let's explore how harnessing this energy can illuminate the path to transformation and deeper connections.

> "Whatever reality you find yourself in
> is capable of being altered by you at any time you want.
> It is not altered by changing what is outside of you;
> it's altered by changing how you choose to process your life."
> —Dr. Wayne Dyer, *The Power of Intention*

Thoughts Do, in Fact, Reach Out Into Your World

Have you ever wondered, "What is a thought?"

A thought is a belief that influences energy, positively or negatively, all the time.

Our thoughts and mental images have an energy to them, which is *set in motion* by an inner attitude. This *energy in motion* instantaneously influences our emotions, resulting in outward behavior, words, and actions which affect our relationships and the people in the world.

We each have the ability to manage our thinking. When we go about it deliberately and with great intention, we can direct our "thought energy" to have more of what we want and less of what we don't want.

Once you understand what scientific research has to teach us about our energy and our "vibes," you will naturally begin to make adjustments that will immediately improve your experiences.

The science we'll cover in this book suggests that we are all connected (capable of being instinctual or intuitive) to whatever degree we allow ourselves to know what we know and feel what we feel.

When we deny this and wall off the world, we also wall off our capacity to know ourselves. We miss out on letting ourselves own our real personal power and acknowledge our connection with others on a meaningful, energetic level.

In the following pages, we will examine a variety of my favorite experiments that illustrate that the mind or consciousness is not restricted to our bodies or to any kind of locality.

Why is this important?

Because what you think matters above and beyond what you may have considered up to this point.

It can have everything to do with why you and your child or you and a classroom of students are struggling so much.

To the school administrator, it can have everything to do with why your faculty and staff are problematic for you and for the children they keep sending to your office.

As we explore the energetic connections that weave through our experiences, we must recognize that these moments of intuition and awareness serve as a window into a deeper understanding of our electromagnetic nature.

Sensing someone's gaze, receiving a call from someone just as you think of them, or feeling an instinctive urge to check on a loved one illustrates how interconnected we truly are.

These seemingly extraordinary occurrences are not merely coincidences; they highlight the ongoing flow of energy and information that exists between individuals.

By tuning into these experiences, we can open ourselves to a broader perception of reality and recognize our subtle influences on one another and our environment.

This understanding lays the groundwork for our
exploration of the science of interconnectedness.
We will examine how our bodies are not only
electric but also magnetic, creating bioenergy fields
around us and ultimately revealing the profound
connections that link all consciousness.

As we transition from understanding how our thoughts extend into the world around us, we will delve deeper into the science behind these connections. Exploring our energetic influence is not merely conceptual; it is grounded in scientific principles that showcase our electromagnetic nature.

Embracing our electromagnetic essence can enhance our awareness of how our thoughts and feelings resonate beyond ourselves, shaping not only our individual experiences but also the dynamics of our relationships and communities.

Next, we will uncover the remarkable ways our bodies operate as living electromagnetic fields. This knowledge elevates our insight into how our thoughts and emotions resonate within ourselves and across the vast tapestry of relationships and environments we inhabit.

Let's now examine how electromagnetic energy and consciousness intertwine, ultimately revealing the profound impact our thoughts have on our reality.

CHAPTER 6

THE POWER OF THOUGHT: UNVEILING THE SENDER-RECEIVER CONNECTION

Imagine a world where thoughts and intentions transcend physical barriers, where the power of one person's mind can influence the neurophysiological responses of another—even from afar.

What unfolds from our first three experiments challenges our understanding of perception and connection, inviting us to consider the energetic threads that bind us together, even when separated by walls.

Hold onto your hat as we explore these experiments, which could reveal insights that transform how we view the power of intention in our lives and interactions from this point forward.

A USER-FRIENDLY INTRODUCTION TO
QUANTUM FIELD THEORY AND INTERCONNECTEDNESS

Experiment #1: Intention-Influence

The historic "Intention-Influence" experiment, by the Institute of Noetic Sciences (IONS), demonstrated a correlation between energy sent and energy received. IONS, founded in 1973 by former Apollo astronaut Edgar Mitchell, is dedicated to the scientific examination of consciousness and interconnectedness.

This nonprofit research organization explores the intersection of science and profound human experience, making it a cutting-edge space for groundbreaking studies like the one on intention and influence.

Revealing the Power of Thought

This experiment is also known as the "Sender-Receiver."

One participant (Subject A) sat in one room connected to a polygraph machine, while another participant (B) remained in a room down the hall.

A polygraph, better known as a lie detector test, measures physiological responses to stress, such as heart rate, blood pressure, and galvanic skin response. When a person experiences stress at any level inside their body, the polygraph machine records it.

Subject B (sender) was instructed to think thoughts that were either "upsetting" or "happy." When she began a new thought, she would push a button to enter the precise time the thought occurred into the computer.

Different buttons designated different types of thoughts—happy or upsetting.

The computer data showing the specific type and timing of each of B's thoughts was then compared to A's (receiver) polygraph results.

The results were nothing short of astonishing.

With repeated experiments, researchers observed an average 90-95% accurate correlation between Subject B's thoughts and the physiological responses recorded on Subject A's polygraph machine readings.

Yes, you read that right!

By using the polygraph, we move beyond conscious knowledge about what might be happening, and we can measure what the body itself just resonated.

This verifies that the power of focused intention is not just a feel-good idea; it's backed by empirical evidence that highlights a tangible connection between individuals, even when separated by distance.

What does this mean for you?

Understanding that your thoughts carry profound energetic influence empowers you to cultivate affirmative intentions in your daily interactions. Imagine turning a conflictual situation (a power struggle) into a productive and collaborative one (a synergistic outcome) by simply shifting your attitude, vibe, and tone!

We can conclude here that thought frequencies are not restricted to our bodies, nor are they restricted to any locality.

What you think matters.

And what you think is felt, seen, heard, and sensed. We are in fact co-mingling our energies all day every day, whether we mean to be or not.

Let's unpack this first experiment:

This first experiment is important because it underscores the realization that thoughts and intentions are not merely abstract phenomena; they carry energetic frequencies that can profoundly influence others.

Which brings us back to our starting point:

You Can't Have An Attitude and Keep It A Secret!

Suppose that you have students or a child in your care that you do not like. In that case, your thought, belief, or emotion toward them creates energy, which influences a physiological response in the child.

While they may not be consciously aware of your energy, they are most likely reacting to it in their behavior.

You've heard the saying, "All behavior is a form of communication."

We are learning to understand how energetics impact behavior and what the behavior is trying to say. Embracing the power of energy can help us decipher the underlying messages behind behaviors.

Let's examine another quantum interconnectedness experiment.

We've all heard this before: "Talk to your plants and they'll grow healthier." But what happens to a plant if it gets bullied?

IKEA wanted answers to that question, so in 2018 they conducted a plant bullying experiment to raise awareness about this very important issue.

Experiment #2: IKEA

IKEA installed two of its Dracaena plants at a school. The children took part in recording compliments to one plant and disparaging words to the other. After 30 days, the bullied plant started to show signs of wilting, while the complimented plant flourished.

As part of the controlled study, both plants received the same physical treatment with water, sunlight, soil, and fertilizer. The only difference was the energy of the thoughts and words they received.

Pretty impressive, right?

Are you skeptical about the so-called science behind the experiment?

You may not know this, but plant experimentation has been going on since the 1950's. Regardless of how crazy it seems, plants are able to produce measurable electrical activity. Other experiments show that plants have primary perception and do, in fact, react to being hit or abused when tracked on a polygraph machine. Check out Peter Tompkins' book *The Secret Life of Plants* for more.

So that brings up another question: Do plants have brains?

Let's defer to neuroscientist Greg Gage, who answers the question by saying, "Plants don't have brains, no axons, no neurons, but what they do have is something very similar to us, which is the ability to communicate using electricity. It uses slightly different ions than we do but it's doing the same thing."

This remarkable ability of plants to interact vibrationally invites us to explore another fascinating experiment that further demonstrates the impact of energy and intention—this time in the world of water and crystals. Let's dive into our next experiment.

Experiment #3: Dr. Emoto's Water and Rice

Through the 1990s, Dr. Emoto conducted a series of experiments observing the physical effects of words, prayers, music, and environment on the crystalline structure of water.

By placing cooked rice and water in glass jars and subjecting them to various verbal stimuli over 30 days, Emoto discovered that thoughts and spoken words could alter the rice's condition, showcasing the profound impact of our vibrations on a molecular level.

In these experiments, the rice became a tangible representation of this phenomenon.

When subjected to positive affirmations such as "thank you," "love," and "you are wonderful," the rice remained relatively fresh and white, reflecting a state of vitality.

Conversely, the rice that endured negative remarks like "you fool," "I hate you," or even silence began to discolor, rot, and emit foul odors.

This visible degradation illustrated the rice's response to the energy of the thoughts and intentions directed at it.

Dr. Emoto's groundbreaking water and rice experiment demonstrated how words and intentions could influence the molecular structure of water—essentially a reminder of how our voice and thoughts carry through the glass jar into the water, prompting a response from the rice.

This finding is particularly important because the human body is roughly 60% water, underscoring the need to consider how our verbal and mental environments shape our well-being.

The point of first leaning into replicable, evidence-based science is to not minimize the energetic significance of what is real and happening, particularly when we face challenges that seem to spiral out of control.

To effectively turn things around, we must be willing to address the heart of the struggle.

Making an energetic connection is what matters most in transforming intense situations.

This approach can empower today's youth to cultivate long-term self-regulation and adept self-advocacy skills, fostering their development and resilience as they navigate the complexities of life.

Let's put this all together!

Our first three experiments illuminate the profound impact of our thoughts and intentions on the world around us.

The "Sender-Receiver" experiment demonstrates a remarkable correlation between one person's thoughts and remote person's neurophysiological—mind-body—responses.

With a 90-95% accuracy rate, these results underscore that thought frequencies transcend individual barriers, influencing others even across distances.

Similarly, the IKEA plant experiment illustrates how the vibrational energy of language and emotion can affect living organisms. The bullied plant, exposed to the vibes of hurtful words, withered in contrast to its complimented counterpart, emphasizing the energetic interplay between expression and growth.

Lastly, Dr. Emoto's water and rice experiment demonstrates how the vibrations of negative or positive thoughts and spoken words can alter the crystalline structure of water, suggesting that our intentions resonate deeply within the molecular realm.

Something To Think About

Collectively, these experiments invite us to recognize the significance of our energetic connections, which shape not only our personal experiences but also impact others and the world at large.

Understanding that our thoughts carry weight empowers us to cultivate affirmative intentions and create a nurturing environment. By doing so, we can develop self- and co-regulatory skills and advocate for ourselves and the youth around us, fostering a supportive community rooted in awareness and respect for the energy we share.

As we continue, it becomes crucial to understand how external influences shape our internal experiences, particularly through the energetic interactions we have with others.

The experiments discussed thus far have illuminated the intricate connections between thought, intention, and energy.

Next, we will focus on how intentionally transmitting calm can elicit measurable neurophysiological responses. This exploration will deepen our understanding of energy dynamics and emphasize our responsibility in inadvertently participating in what's happening whether we mean to be not.

By examining these energetic interactions, we can better comprehend their implications on well-being and development, especially in our increasingly interconnected world.

CHAPTER 7

THE INVISIBLE THREADS OF INFLUENCE

As we're discovering, the power of thought extends far beyond our individual experiences and relationships, influencing even the most unexpected elements of our environment.

Consider the groundbreaking experiments into the interconnectedness of consciousness, which demonstrate how our intentions, emotions, and beliefs can affect everything from a simple plant to the very fabric of our interactions with others.

These studies illustrate that what we think truly matters. From the ability to influence emotional states over distances, to a scientist's conversation with a cactus, each reveals the profound impact that our intentions can have on the world.

By embracing this understanding, we empower ourselves to optimize our relationships and enhance our overall well-being.

Picking up where we left off, let's delve into the fascinating connections between our thoughts and their implications for our lives.

Experiment #4: Distant Mental Influence

In a groundbreaking experiment in 1983 exploring calming mental influence at a distance, researchers William Braud, PhD. and Marilyn Schlitz, PhD. demonstrated that influencers can successfully transmit a calming effect to subjects without any sensory communication. The study investigated the concept of energetic interconnectedness among humans, leveraging the ability to influence emotional states over distances.

Conducted under strict conditions, the influencers and the subjects were separated by a distance of 20 meters in soundproof rooms, thereby eliminating any potential sensory distractions or communications. The subjects were cushioned in comfort with soothing sounds and abstract visuals while having no prior knowledge of the experiment's objectives or timeline.

The subjects' level of stress and agitation was assessed using a lie detector-like system that measured changes in skin electrical activity, indicative of nervous system responses. The influencers alternated between periods of focused mental concentration aimed at projecting calmness and periods of disengagement from the subjects' states of agitation. This strategic approach allowed researchers to assess whether the influencers' mental efforts produced significant physiological changes in the agitated subjects.

The results were compelling: significant reductions in subjects' stress levels during the influencers' calming periods confirmed a strong mental connection between individuals, demonstrating the ability of mental intention to positively affect others across distances. This experiment illuminates the mechanisms of energetic interconnectedness and their implications for emotional well-being.

Experiment #5: Corn Plant Experiment

A similar result was obtained by Cleve Backster, who is one of the foremost experts in the polygraph. As far back as twenty-five years ago, he liked to share the story about the time he was working with a polygraph machine in his laboratory late one night when he decided to take a break and make a cup of instant coffee. As he waited for the water to boil, curiosity made him wonder, "Gee, what would happen if I wired up the polygraph to the corn plant in the corner of my office?"

He placed electrodes around the corn plant and then began to think what he could do to stress or scare the plant, to try to elicit a stress response on the polygraph. He decided that scorching a leaf would surely cause anxiety in the plant. So, he found some matches and stood beside the plant. As he took a match out of the box, intending to strike it and burn the plant, the polygraph made a sound of response. Backster was startled by the noise—he hadn't yet lit the match—and he assumed there must be some misconnection. He then examined the plant and found that the electrodes were solidly placed, with nothing out of order.

Once again, he took the match and held it in his hand, and again, at the very moment he had the intention to strike the match to burn the leaf of the plant, the polygraph reacted dramatically. By this time his water was boiling, and he went to the kettle to make his cup of instant coffee. But as he poured the remaining water down the drain of the sink, the polygraph reacted again, and this time he was doubly surprised. He thought, "What's going on now?"

He boiled more water, but when he poured it down the drain, the polygraph did not react. After speaking to a biologist friend about it, they concluded that when the scientist poured the boiling water down the drain the first time, the corn plant was reacting to the stress of other living cells—bacteria in the sink that were killed by the hot water. However, when he poured it down the second time, the bacteria had already been killed. The scientists hypothesized that there was a connected resonance between the bacteria in the sink and the corn plant. The interconnectedness of mind, or of consciousness, throughout our world is something that stands out strikingly to us.

The Power of Energetic Communication

Experiment #6: Spineless Cactus

Luther Burbank, the famous botanist, conducted a very interesting experiment. He developed many different species of plants, and one of his goals was to develop a spineless cactus. He would take a cactus and remove its spines, to see if it would live and then be reproduced as a spineless cactus. Each time he did that, the plant would die. He replicated the experiment several times without success.

Then one day, being an energy-minded person himself, he had a thought—he would talk to his plant. He assured the cactus that he would take very good care of the plant here in his laboratory, that there would be no harm, there would be no animals or any other creatures that could come in to harm the cactus, even without its spines. And with that, he removed the spines from the cactus. This time the cactus lived, and Burbank was able to reproduce spineless cacti.

Psychologists have slowly picked up on the relevance of quantum theory to their practice. The traditional medical community has begun to accept these theories and incorporate them into the medical model of healing.

I say it's "begun" only because many of today's scientists, including those in the field of medicine, still function within the old Newtonian paradigm. It is easier for these practitioners to ignore the new findings and to continue to rely on the logical and rational models they were originally trained in. As we look at some of the findings of quantum mechanical experiments, you will see that they seem to turn logic and rationality upside-down.

Something To Think About

Connecting the dots between these three experiments uncovers a profound truth:

> Our thoughts, intentions, and emotional states
> have far-reaching effects that extend
> beyond our immediate experience.

Braud and Schlitz's work illustrates the power of distant mental influence, demonstrating that calmness can be transmitted without direct interaction. Backster's corn plant experiment showcases that even plants possess a sensitivity to human intentions. And Burbank's successful development of a spineless cactus shows the significance of intentional energy in fostering growth.

This insight encourages us to take responsibility for our thoughts and feelings, understanding that they can shape our relationships and influence our surroundings.

By harnessing this awareness, we can foster more constructive interactions and cultivate a reality that reflects our highest intentions, ultimately empowering us to create meaningful change in our lives.

There's more!

CHAPTER 8

EVIDENCE OF SUB-ATOMIC COMMUNICATION

In our exploration of consciousness and connectivity, we now delve into compelling evidence of sub-atomic communication.

Recent experiments observes that particles originating from the same atomic mass maintain an instantaneous connection, regardless of distance. This astonishing phenomenon suggests that we are constantly interacting with our environment at a fundamental level.

Coupled with findings on the energy of thoughts and emotions, we come to understand that our intentions can influence not only our lives but also the lives of others, transcending physical boundaries.

Now, let's uncover the profound implications of these experiments and what they clarify about our interconnected reality.

Experiment #7: Sub-atomic Communication

In 1969, physicists proved that sub-atomic particles which originated from a common atom continued to experience a kind of communication with each other that kept them permanently in touch with each other regardless of distance.

The way this was tested was to split an atom apart and manipulate the magnetic polarity—the "spin"—of a pair of separated electrons. They found that the pair of electrons would always spin in opposite directions from each other, due to their opposite magnetic polarity. If they reversed the direction of spin of one electron, then the spin of the other electron reversed instantaneously.

Furthermore, physicists proved that the relationship of opposite spin is maintained by both electrons at a distance of 20 feet apart. By the end of the 20th century, hundreds of experiments had increased the distance to halfway around the world and the results were confirmed, regardless of the distance between the paired electrons.

Scientists were able to document that the two electrons, originating from the same atomic mass, switched direction at precisely the same moment that the manipulation of one was initiated! This observed phenomenon is called quantum entanglement.

This demonstrates that sub-atomic matter is constantly and consistently reading its environment and communicating over immense distances.

Further Possibilities of Energy and Distance

Experiment #8: Energy and Distance

This basic knowledge of electromagnetic energy communication was once again the impetus for experimenter Cleve Backster to further examine the possibilities of energy and distance.

Backster wanted to prove that we have the power to send energy over a long distance through characteristics that are present in atomic mass, which includes the structure and behavior of electrons.

He set up an experiment in which he scraped cells from the inside of the mouth of an actor and put the cells in a petri dish. The actor then drove to another laboratory seven miles away. His assignment was to act angry at certain intervals.

At exactly the instant the actor began to act angry, the electrical activity in the cells in the petri dish changed. Before that moment, the cells in the petri dish were showing very little electrical activity.

In fact, the electronic survey only registered that there were cells there, and the petri dish was not empty. Yet the more invested the actor became in experiencing anger, the greater the level of electrical activity in the cells present in the petri dish.

Now let's look at these two experiments together:

The first experiment suggests we are all part of an incredible and pervasive communication system in which distance is irrelevant.

The second experiment suggests that thoughts have energy that magnetizes electrons, measurable by electrical activity in living cells, again at a distance.

From this we can surmise that intentional thought energy may be transmitted instantaneously over a distance, like a radio station to a receiver.

This is precisely how we create our experiences in the physical world and within ourselves and each other.

These experiments illustrate that our thoughts and intentions not only transmit energy over vast distances but also forge deep connections beyond our immediate surroundings.

A compelling example of this phenomenon in action can be found in our next story where an aboriginal hunter telepathically contacts his tribe in moments of need, showcasing how shared consciousness facilitates remarkable understanding and collaboration.

Message Sending, Message Receiving

Dr. E. Page Bailey, creator of *Educotherapy*, offers his explanation of this in his program, *Pathways to Accelerated Recovery from Chronic Pain*:

Atoms are universal, and at the atomic level there is energy in us that's in all the universe. But we are not sharing electrons, we are modifying electron behavior in each other or in the outcome of events. Our electrons are reading other electrons as we are moving empathetically.

For example, telepathy is really just the electromagnetic information that we are receiving. Receptive people are simply open to the translation of those energies which are present around them. And there can be no question about the fact that some people have a special receptivity, and that through exercise they have developed it to very high levels.

We are all receptive at some level. In Marlo Morgan's book, *Mutant Message Down Under*, she has a chapter called *Cordless Phone*. There is a passage in which one of the hunters has left the tribe and goes out to kill a kangaroo. He does so, but drinks contaminated water, becomes ill and contacts the tribe telepathically. Morgan observes the tribe suddenly stopping in their daily trek.

They kneel quietly and receive the message that the hunter is asking for permission to bring the kangaroo to a predetermined destination in the desert, which itself is a fascinating process: how do they determine position in the desert—how do they do that?

The tribe could not have picked up just any message. If that brave hunter with the kangaroo said, "I want tickets to see the Ravens football game," the tribe would not have gotten that message.

There is a pre-conditioned message sending and message receiving set that has been created in the culture. This aboriginal tribe has developed receptivity to a particular set of messages.

Now we in our culture have also created receptivity to a certain set of messages in the human dialogic process, and those messages are again determined by pre-conditioning.

Let's say that you are in a conversation with someone and you find yourself saying:

"Tell me what you told me again. I know you just said some words but give me more words so that I'm sure what your words meant."

What you may be sensing intuitively is that there is another script and other material that has not yet been said out loud. That intuition would not be there if there were not a message sending and receiving process.

This can happen when we are first beginning to date someone, especially if we are very interested in the person, but we are not verbalizing that yet.

Or you may be in a conversation, and you hear just a few words, but you intuit many more, and you are troubled by the fact that you did not get to confirm your intuition.

Another way to describe this is the message conditioning that the culture has provided for us, and we are all receptive to cultural messages to different degrees and in different ways.

You may be asking, "Does this mean I can get my thoughts and thus my energy all over you?" Yes it can, whether you mean for it to be happening or not.

For now, let's move on to another very exciting experiment which uncovers how thoughts influence energy and outcome.

Something To Think About

Let's tie these two experiments on energy transmission over distance together with the compelling example of the hunter and his tribe.

These observations all together suggest that our thoughts and emotions may transcend time and space, forging connections that influence others, even from afar.

Just as the split electrons and anger influencing cells demonstrated instantaneous communication, the hunter's telepathic link to his tribe illustrates the powerful potential of shared consciousness.

This understanding empowers us to be more intentional with our thoughts, recognizing that they may impact not only our relationships but also connect us to a broader human experience.

By harnessing this ability, we can cultivate deeper connections and create beneficial changes in our lives and communities.

CHAPTER 9

THE QUANTUM CONNECTION

Thoughts that Shape Reality

What if our understanding of the universe shifted drastically because of how we observe it?

The groundbreaking Wheeler Delayed Choice Experiment fundamentally challenges our perception of reality, demonstrating that our intentions and expectations can shape the behavior of subatomic particles.

When electrons are scrutinized, they can behave as particles or waves based solely on the observer's expectations, revealing a fascinating truth: our thoughts wield immense power.

As we explore this next experiment, we'll uncover how our perceptions impact not just the subatomic realm, but also the young minds we nurture, empowering us to create transformative connections in our lives and the lives of others.

Experiment #9: Wheeler Delayed Choice

What if I told you that our understanding of the universe began to unravel in the 1970s as scientists harnessed a groundbreaking technology that could propel electrons closer to the speed of light than ever before?

A new technology allowed scientists to fire electrons at a series of gates and sensors that could detect their behaviors as they passed through.

When they would fire the electrons at a screen with two apertures, they were amazed to find that the electrons, which were believed to be particles, would sometimes behave like electromagnetic energy waves.

Sometimes, the electrons would go through the top aperture, and sometimes they'd go through the bottom aperture.

Sometimes, the electrons would change into a light wave that goes through both apertures, converges on the other side, and becomes a particle again.

What happened at the second set of gates and sensors was baffling. The sensor could be calibrated to count electrons or waves, and they could change from one mode to the other *after* each electron had *already passed* through the first gate and sensor.

When they looked for particles (expectation), they found 100% particles, whether they had been measured as a particle or a wave at the first gate.

When they looked for waves (expectation) in the same experiment, they found 100% waves.

 CHANGE YOUR VIBE, SEE YOUR KIDS THRIVE

These results occurred without regard to the fact that the decision as to which state they were looking for was made *after* each electron had *already* passed through the first gate and sensor. Hence the name "Delayed Choice" Experiment.

The scientists at first could not make sense of how this happened.

Finally, after extensive experimentation and research, they recognized that the only variable that determined the way the electron would behave was the observation method chosen (expectation) by the experimenter.

> For the first time in scientific history,
> it was recognized that an experimental result was
> solely dependent on the expectation of the experimenter.
> Given that fact, any life experience could be
> influenced by the way you expect it to unfold.

Electrons constantly and consistently read their environment and act as expected, changing to pure energy—or remaining solid, i.e. thoughts continually affect electrons by intent (expectation). This proven result defies the known laws of physics.

One possible implication from these findings is that our intention (expectation) is transmitted directly into our environment, and the electromagnetic energy of electrons reacts to the infinitesimal signals we send.

So, what we think, believe, intend, have faith in, and expect all have energy that flows out of us and may be "read" by our physical environment.

Electrons are responding in kind to the thoughts we hold in mind.

Why is this important in loving, living, and working with today's children?

We've just revealed a fascinating fact: your thoughts and intentions are not just whispers in the wind. Given what we know from the experiments described in the preceding chapters, it is quite possible that, perhaps through quantum entanglement, your thoughts and intentions may be powerful forces directly influencing the neurological, physiological, and emotional landscape of the young minds around you and in your care.

Imagine the potential transformation when you realize that your expectations can either uplift a child's spirit or trigger unexpected emotional responses.

> Nothing is anything until you call it!
> If you call whatever is happening in your life
> right now a success, you will be energized by
> the opportunity smack-dab in front of you.
> - Mary Robinson Reynolds

Something To Think About

As we conclude the scientific inquiry into how we are all interconnected, it's vital to recognize that the implications of our thoughts, intentions, and actions extend far beyond ourselves. They ripple outward, co-mingling with the thoughts, experiences, emotions, and behaviors of the children we encounter daily.

The insights from this experiment remind us that, similarly to the particles in a quantum experiment, children's energetic, neurophysiological, and emotional realities are influenced by the infusion of our perceptions and expectations.

Why not always hold happy outcomes in your mind, heart, and spirit? As you can see, it has an automatic impact on your nervous system.

These scientific concepts can inform practical tools that can help us nurture resilience, foster confidence, and inspire genuine connections.

Consider this: every interaction with a child is an opportunity to send a powerful message.

What kind of energetic messaging are you sending—infusing the child with?

A quick example is the parent who drops their kid off at school and then worries and ruminates.

> It's been said that "worry" is like
> giving energy to everything you do not want.

Realize now that this is, in fact, being transmitted to those around us, whether you mean for it to be or not!

Worrying is energy, as is fear. Over time—and often in real-time—it is transmitted to the child. The unspoken message is clear: based on the child's problematic behaviors, you don't trust them and you expect them to mess up. This expectation leads to situations where you are repeatedly called back to school to pick them up or other similar scenarios that have been playing out in your lives.

If you habitually think these "worry thoughts," chances are that you are putting emotion and upset right alongside those thoughts. Worry is what's being transmitted, and over time, there is a buildup, and emotional upsets become more and more frequent.

What you can do is this:

Visualize best case scenarios. Ask yourself if you are energetically uplifting, supportive, and encouraging, or are you overlooking the unspoken struggles the child may face. What skills do they need to learn and be coached on?

I'll never forget the first time a mother I was working with said, "You mean all I have to do is visualize a good outcome?"

I said, "Yes!" without blinking an eye.

She was skeptical but willing to try anything at that point.

Guess what happened?

Sure enough, at our next group meeting, she came in happy, relieved, and excited to share an amazing win for her child in what could otherwise have become a tough situation.

The choice is yours. By consciously embracing compassion, empathy, and awareness in our communication, we can create environments that dissolve barriers, celebrate individuality and ignite the passion for learning.

> What you think about repeatedly,
> consistently fueled with emotion,
> comes about either negatively or positively.

So, let's tap into the energy in our role as educators, mentors, and caregivers.

Interrupt yourself at the thought level.

Shift your focus from worst-case scenarios to the inspiring potential of best-case outcomes. It's just as easy to visualize best-case as worst-case scenarios.

Start by being mindful of how you observe and interact with the children in your life. You may be thinking: "This child is trying to make my life miserable." To instantly change your vibe, think this instead: "This child's life is miserable. Now, what can I do to help, not harm?"

Make it a practice to be aware of your thoughts and intentions, and use them to uplift those around you.

Share stories of resilience and growth, and foster open dialogues where children feel safe expressing the thoughts they were thinking that stirred up their emotions.

By committing to this path, we influence young minds and engage in a powerful connection that can transform lives, spark growth, and shape a brighter future. Let's harness the power of our intentions to empower every child we meet. The future is brimming with potential—let's ignite it together!

Energetics isn't just about theory; it's a call to action!

Something To Think About

As we wrap up our exploration of quantum physics experiments, let's shift our focus toward the intricate dance of energies that exists between us and our children.

Just as particles are in quantum entanglement and constantly in motion, children's behaviors often reflect our thoughts and emotions, mirroring our state of being. This reciprocal relationship provides us with a unique opportunity to assess and realign our intentions.

Embrace the idea that our energy influences their responses, and remember that our mindful interactions can create an atmosphere ripe for growth and productivity.

So, as we move forward, let's delve deeper into how this co-mingling of energies may influence behavior in our classrooms and homes, illuminating the path for a transformative approach to understanding and nurturing our children's development.

Together, we can turn this reflection into a powerful catalyst for change!

Co-Mingling, Barometers, and Mirrors ... Oh My!

CHAPTER 10

CO-MINGLING ENERGIES

Energy is Not Contagious; We Are Simply Co-Mingling!

Have you ever walked into a room and instantly felt its emotional atmosphere? It's as if an invisible energy envelope surrounds you. That sensation isn't just your imagination; it's called energetic co-mingling.

This is the fascinating dance of energetic co-mingling—a phenomenon that shapes the mood of your family, classroom, or school dynamic.

So, what exactly is energetic co-mingling?

It occurs when your emotional energy mixes, merges, and infuses with those around you, creating a swirl of vibrations that influences everyone involved. This blend can either enhance harmony or lead to an emotional earthquake.

Think of it as the way we blend our emotional energies: each family member brings their unique vibes; some days might feel like a perfect smoothie, while other days could feel like a chaotic mess.

When we co-mingle, one person's vibes can either uplift a group or bring it crashing down.

For instance, picture yourself enjoying a cheerful afternoon with your child, only to be blindsided by a sudden wave of dread. That feeling could stem from your partner's rough day at work—proof that emotional energy is as real and transmissible as any physical force.

How a person is neurologically wired through their personality style can greatly determine their receptivity to the energies of others. (Learn how at: ConnectingWithColors.com for actionable insights.)

Understanding this dynamic can help prevent conflicts from escalating. Ultimately, energetically infused emotions are like wireless signals—they broadcast loudly even if we're not aware of them.

The Art of Co-Mingling

Imagine this scenario: you're having a productive day at work when a knot in your stomach prompts concern about one of your children. Later, when they come home from school, you discover they had been bullied around that same time, and their emotional turmoil was echoing through the bond between the two of you.

Energy operates like a wireless signal—strong yet invisible—transmitting emotionally triggering waves that shape your feelings and reactions. This subtle influence can affect your mood and interactions without you even realizing it.

Recognizing how energy flows between you and your loved ones enables you to resolve conflicts before they escalate.

By being aware of your environment, you can become a proactive energy manager.

As Dr. Murray Bowen described in, *Family Systems Theory*, family systems are intricate webs where one person's mood can ripple through the entire household. He emphasizes understanding individuals through their emotional interactions.

If you've had a happy day but your spouse walks in angry and on edge, those negative vibes can ripple through your household. Energy can quickly become chaotic and irritating, especially during family dinners disrupted by sibling rivalries or a refusal to eat.

Cloe Madanes and Dr. Jay Haley further developed this idea, in *Strategic Family Therapy*, noting that what we label as "symptoms" often reflect deeper systemic issues within families.

I recall attending a workshop led by these two brilliant minds; their idea that dysfunction could be understood through the lens of behavioral symptoms completely changed my perspective and healed a significant part of my childhood.

Upon digesting this concept, I realized how I had absorbed my mother's unfulfilled dreams, unknowingly taking on the role of PC: "Problem Child," fulfilling her unmet desire to be a schoolteacher.

I'll never forget the year my mother got to substitute teach for two months. I did great. I enjoyed having her put her energies toward other kids and stop helicoptering me.

Awareness of these dynamics is an advantage; it means we don't need to carry others' agitating energies. A simple acknowledgment of each other's feelings can create a profoundly supportive environment.

The good news is that we don't have to carry the burden of others' "tough day" energies. By doing a compassionate check-in—such as acknowledging our loved one's intense day—you can prevent lingering negativity from taking over family interactions.

Transparency fosters a supportive atmosphere, allowing everyone to align and tackle opportunities together.

Your emotional state doesn't belong to anyone else to carry for you (i.e., shoulder your emotional burdens). When you prioritize self-care, your energy is effortless, uplifting those around you without even trying.

Open dialogues and joyful activities can transform a heavy room into a place of light and joy.

Here are just a few riveting stories about how children carry symptoms for their families, and how they finally got resolved.

Guilt

A mother arrived at my office concerned about her son's sudden disruptive behavior at school. Instead of jumping to conclusions, I used my *What, If, When Method* (Part II) to uncover the emotional dynamics at play. It turned out she was wrestling with the decision to return to work, feeling immense guilt and anxiety. By addressing her energy, we helped shift the dynamics at home, alleviating the burden her son was carrying. His behavior improved within several days.

Infidelity

In another instance, a family sought help for their troubled teenage son, who felt betrayed by his father's infidelity. He had begun getting into trouble at school, a behavior that was unlike him. By addressing the parents' issues, we alleviated some of the emotional burdens on the son, allowing him to reclaim his emotional space.

Depression

Then there was the eight year old boy who was repeatedly setting fires, trying desperately to draw attention to the deep struggle in his home life. His risky and reckless behavior was a cry for help masked in chaos, stemming from a mother mired in suicidal depression. This story illustrates not just the difficulty associated with co-mingling energies but the necessity of addressing root causes with outside help such as social services or family therapy.

The link between a child's distress and a parent's energetic state infusing the emotional climate can be startlingly clear.

Alcoholism

Consider a girl battling severe anorexia, whose struggles were closely intertwined with her father's alcoholism—a topic he avoided like the plague. It wasn't until family therapy prompted him to confront the consequences of his addiction that meaningful progress began to unfold. As they learned how the co-mingling of energies was affecting the daughter, healing became possible for the entire family.

Each of these narratives shines a light on a profound experience: children can bear the weight of energetically infused, emotional family dynamics if they are left unchecked and unresolved.

These stories are just a glimpse into how understanding energetic co-mingling can transform lives. It can be unproductive, even counter-productive to label behavior as right or wrong, good or bad.

Likewise, it may be a misuse of time, resources, and financial investment to start by diagnosing a child's "personality disorders," categorizing symptoms and opening the DSM-5 before examining the relationships among the adults and siblings in the home or school. Often, one can view behavior simply as a symptom of the co-mingling energies of family dynamics that need attention.

So, the next time you feel the emotional tides rising, remember—you hold the power to change the energy landscape around you, transforming chaos into connection one interaction at a time!

Understand that your energy impacts those around you, whether you're at home, at school, or in the community. A warm, welcoming attitude invites connection, and every shared smile or laugh is a chance to uplift the atmosphere.

CHAPTER 11

THE SILENT INDICATORS

Dancing with Energy at Home, School, and Beyond

Kids Are Our Barometers

Understanding children as barometers—sensitive instruments gauging the emotional pressure in their environments—allows us to see their behaviors in a different light. How often do we, as parents or educators, misinterpret a child's outburst as mere defiance rather than looking for the underlying emotional signal?

Kids, with their innate sense of emotional acuity, absorb the energy around them. If you're feeling anxious about finances, that tension can seep into your child's well-being.

An everyday situation—such as putting away shoes—can trigger a complete meltdown due to the energetic pressure of unresolved stress running in the background. They aren't spoiled; they're responding to the energetic climate, feeling the agitation in the air. Pause before labeling them as difficult or disrespectful. They might be reacting to stressors you're unaware of.

For instance, consider the parent who thinks they have better things to do than reason with their child, let alone understand their child's resistance to following a directive.By pausing for just 30 seconds to uncover what's driving that behavior, they could address the heart of the issue. Instead of compounding it with a time-out, which, at best, doesn't resolve anything or teach any skills, they could nurture a more constructive relationship.

How do we address this? Instead of delving straight into what a child is feeling when they act out, I recommend simply doing a *Quickie Vibe Check-In*. Go get it at: MaryReynolds.com/Gifts

The Tone of the Home

An openly chaotic atmosphere or a subversively quiet one, both charged with emotionally triggering energy, is like a pressure gauge; it fluctuates and impacts how every family member feels and reacts.

If there's tension between you and your partner, even a minor issue, like a misplaced toy, can set off a child's meltdown, especially if the upset between you has been building over time, permeating the home's energetic landscape.

Moreover, energetic turbulence and unavailability, possibly stemming from an adult's substance abuse, can affect a child's emotional triggers and well-being significantly.

It's no surprise that loud arguments or even a dense silence can send children into chaos or erratic activity.

Imagine this: you and your partner have been snippy with each other, and suddenly your daughter melts down over a less-than-perfect peanut butter and jelly sandwich. She's not being dramatic;

she's giving you a barometric pressure reading on the emotional tension she's being—inadvertently—infused with.

Children are incredibly receptive and perceptive; they sponge up the emotional atmospheric pressure, often acting out the tension through disruptive behaviors.

In contrast to traditional views of child behavior, your child isn't trying to make your life miserable, their life is miserable, and they lack the words to describe their feelings, often reduced to a simple expression of, "it feels icky right now."

What's a kid to do?

Contrary to DARP—Default Adulting Response Patterns—kids don't get up in the morning thinking, "For the fun of it, I'm going to ruin my day by intentionally and deliberately blowing up every adult in my way."

I coined the term DARP to describe the unconscious reactions we often have as adults, shaped by traditionally hurtful tactics we experienced in childhood. These patterns of response can manifest as knee-jerk reactions or defensive behaviors that reflect the coping mechanisms we developed in response to our early experiences.

As a result, DARP can restrict our ability to respond thoughtfully and empathetically to children, as we may unconsciously project our past wounds onto them.

Understanding and recognizing these patterns is crucial for breaking the cycle and fostering healthier interactions. I dive into DARP more deeply in my *MAPit* System Macro-Dose Online Course available at: MaryReynolds.com/MAPit

It's important to remember that children do not know why they are acting the way they do; they simply feel miserable and need to do something to ease the pressure their discomfort.

There often are no accurate words to capture this feeling. Rather than social emotional learning protocols, you don't have to start investigating by asking a child what they are feeling. I think it's great that we're teaching kids how to access their feelings, but if you want to get to the heart of the problem quicker, you can start by finding out what they've been thinking about first. Because incoming energies coupled with thinking is what's creating feelings.

When it comes to engaging with children I like to kick things off by exploring their thoughts with my *What, If, When Method* (Part II).

This technique helps me uncover what's really going on beneath the surface. By asking, "What was the thought?" we can dive right into the heart of the issue, allowing us to gradually articulate feelings that matter.

As we delve deeper, we start to see how thoughts and feelings are intertwined. It's like peeling back the layers of an onion: once we get to the heart of the matter, we can *lean in* to the source of those feelings and truly begin to understand.

This method not only fosters a safe space for kids to express themselves but also cultivates a stronger bond of trust. By prioritizing their thoughts first, we remove any pressure to label emotions, making the conversation feel more organic and less confrontational.

If you're looking to make your conversations with children more impactful and to eliminate excuse-making, I recommend giving this method a try. You might be surprised at how much insight and connection it creates!

 CHANGE YOUR VIBE, SEE YOUR KIDS THRIVE

Upsets in a love relationship, or financial worries, can seep into everyday life, creating invisible emotional weights that children of all ages can sense and may be reactive to.

Moreover, energetic turbulence stemming from depression, anxiety, substance, and alcohol abuse—any kind of addiction, including screens—can dramatically affect a child's emotional triggers and well-being significantly because of the vibes the adult is infusing into the room.

> The emotional unavailability in addiction
> is the absence of energy.

Adults who are addicted to their screens or substances are emotionally—and therefore energetically—unavailable, and that is very scary for children because it feels like abandonment because it is abandonment in a very real and tangible way. It empties a child's cup, so to speak, not fill it. Kids who consistently behave well and peacefully all have "full cups."

The best comparison I can give you about what it's like for a child whose caretakers are energetically and emotionally checked out is to imagine yourself on a plane flying at 35,000 feet. Suddenly, the pilot comes on the intercom and says, "I've just realized I don't know what I'm doing, so, hey, here we are!"

In that moment, you would likely think, "So that's it? We're done for!" followed by a surge of panic and disbelief, along with a profound sense of fear. Just like those passengers, a child in a similar situation grapples with anxiety and confusion, wondering who will provide the love, guidance, and stability they desperately need. It's as if they are adrift in a chaotic world, feeling vulnerable and unsure of what will happen next.

Which brings us to sleep problems! Need a miracle at bedtime? The best place to start is your energy.

Navigating Bedtime Challenges: The Influence of Parental Energetic Availability on Children

Here it is. Stop being in a rush to get on with your evening. Your impatience at bedtime is an unsettling vibe, and it can make children feel unwanted, which takes us back to a pilotless airplane.

Bedtime is the end of the day. It's dark, and it can feel isolating and lonely for a child. In those quiet moments, if a child senses that a parent is disengaged or preoccupied—feeling as though they have better things to do than to invest a little more emotional and energetic presence—this can heighten feelings of loneliness and insecurity.

Important Warning About "Self-Soothing" Techniques: Protect Your Child's Well-being

Let me be clear about the topic of self-soothing: it can be used in ways that may inadvertently harm your child. As with "Tough Love" and "Time Outs," self-soothing techniques can be misapplied by well-meaning parents.

While the intention might be to promote self-reliance or discipline, these misguided applications can leave emotional scars that hinder a child's ability to self-govern effectively later on in life.

Rather than fostering independence, these punitive methods may exacerbate anxiety and insecurity in children. Instead of a beneficial tool, self-soothing can transform into a survival mechanism,

     CHANGE YOUR VIBE, SEE YOUR KIDS THRIVE

potentially leading to harmful behaviors or emotional withdrawal, opening the door to attachment disorders.

Understanding the delicate balance of emotional support and independence is essential as we explore how to foster healthy co- and self-soothing practices without the detrimental effects of harsh parenting techniques.

It's crucial to recognize that certain sleep training methods, such as Ferberizing (allowing your child to "cry it out"), have been scientifically shown to pose serious risks to your child's health and emotional development.

What you may not know is that Richard Ferber, the originator of the method, is not a psychologist and lacks formal training in mental health. His approach may be likened to a layperson trying to perform surgery without the necessary medical education or expertise.

Moreover, children left to cry do not simply experience discomfort; they absorb the absence of emotional support in their environment. If caregivers are emotionally unavailable—due to stress, addiction, or distraction—children sense this energetic turbulence, often interpreting it as abandonment, which may lead to attachment struggles.

Even more alarming, a recent study by Harvard researchers disclosed that infants who are left crying can suffer long-lasting damage to their nervous systems and may be at a greater risk of developing anxiety disorders, including panic attacks, later in life.

The link between rising aggression and anxiety-related issues among teenagers and those who experienced Ferberizing as infants is concerning and must not be ignored.

Dr. Margot Sunderland, the Director of Education and Training at The Centre for Child Mental Health in London, echoes these concerns, asserting that repeated crying without reassurance can lead to suboptimal brain development.

This reinforces the vital importance of emotional availability. If caregivers are energetically checked out—whether due to their struggles with addiction, or preoccupation with screens, or reading novels with their nose in a book all day—the reassuring energy a child needs is absent.

In these tense moments, children feel adrift, much like passengers on a pilotless plane, grappling with anxiety and confusion.

Given this evidence, it is clear that Ferberizing is neither a safe nor effective method of sleep training. I urge you to reconsider any reliance on this technique in order to protect your child's health and emotional well-being.

Emotional Availability Shapes Sleep Experiences

Children thrive on the energy of connection, and when they perceive that a parent is unavailable, it compounds the natural apprehensions that arise as they settle in for the night.

In my personal experience, when I had all the time in the world to give to my son, he'd fall asleep quickly after reading just one book.

However, on the nights that I was anxious to attend to cleaning up, work responsibilities, or adult conversations, it took three, four, and sometimes five books before I surrendered to just BE-ing energetically, emotionally, and physically available for him, and he could fall asleep.

Unexpected Benefits

I am a proponent of bedtime rituals, like a little roughhousing to release any pent up energy of the day, bathing, a small snack if needed, lying down, and reading. If my son had experienced something hurtful or confusing that day, that was the time he would have opened up and talked to me about it.

Because of our bedtime routine and my relaxing into "be here now," it also became a time for him to discuss anything that had been on his mind.

These bedtime rituals not only provided a sense of security but also opened the door to unexpected benefits that shaped his emotional resilience.

Having worked with many children who struggled throughout their lives, I believed that the best way to keep my son safe in this world was to nurture his intuition. Instead of telling him how to solve his hurts and frustrations with other kids or adults, I'd say, "Let's take a moment to think about and imagine a best case scenario"

We'd close our eyes, and then when he was done, I'd ask, "So what did you see?" More often than not, what he had "heard" and "visualized" aligned perfectly with the advice I would have given. I say "would have" because I refrained from directing him at that point.

> My advice to adults is always to stop talking
> and start listening.

By not telling him what to do, I encouraged him to tap into his own intuition and inner guidance, equipping him with tools to evaluate opportunities, especially as he approached the pivotal time of turning sixteen and receiving his car keys.

Having been a high school guidance counselor, I knew all too well the temptations he would encounter in high school, including the pressures of partying and the allure of drugs, sex, and countless other decisions that could create life-defining moments.

This leads me to your 2nd gift resource: the *Jedi Mind Trick*! Be sure to watch my Micro-Dose resource video on exactly how I employed this strategy to keep my son safe throughout his high school and college years.

MaryReynolds.com/Gifts

Today, that foundation continues to keep him safe. He is now a father of two boys, incorporating the same kind and firm adulting and intuitive practices into their lives.

But we're not done yet! There's more you need to know.

CHAPTER 12

MIRROR, MIRROR, ON THE WALL WHAT ARE OUR KIDS SHOWING US ALL?

It is said that all behavior is communication. Often, it conveys a mirror message for us to see ourselves.

Have you ever observed your child's chaotic behavior and wondered if it's reflecting your own internal struggles?

It's much like looking into a funhouse mirror—distorted and confusing. When your child has a meltdown, it might be a signal that you're on the edge of losing it, too.

Imagine a classroom where a teacher transmits warmth, where students likely feel safe and engaged. In contrast, if a teacher is gloomy or irritable, students may respond differently due to their unique ways of processing emotions and energy. These reactions don't mean there's a behavioral disorder but rather reflect each child's personality and neurological wiring. Understanding this dynamic can help foster a more supportive environment for every learner.

I believe the new scientific term for this is "icky" energy!

As we've been discussing, the emotional tone in your home significantly impacts your child's behavior. You may ask, "Why is my child always so angry at me?" or feel as if your adolescent is enveloped in a cloud of hostility.

The question to ask is, "Am I angry about something that I'm vibing and they are mirroring back to me?"

Do your kids fight a lot?

Could it be they are mirroring your relationship with your spouse or other important adults in your life?

Do you have students in your classrooms mirroring your disdain for certain students by doing the same?

As parents and educators, we often cling to the "do as I say, not as I do" mantra, but let's unpack that.

If your child is upset over something minor, like a missing toy, could it be a reflection of your stress about adult responsibilities?

Children absorb the energy around them, tuning into the "Anxiety Station"—a metaphor for how they resonate with adult stress and worries—when we are preoccupied with our burdens.

Our beliefs and attitudes shape family dynamics in profound ways.

Another unexpected reaction from children can come when you cheerfully encourage your kids with a bright, "You can do this!" Yet, if beneath that enthusiasm lies a current of self-doubt, your children will pick up on it.

Their behavior often mirrors that uncertainty. It's essential, then, to do a *Quickie Vibe Check-List* review with yourself and resolve your

     CHANGE YOUR VIBE, SEE YOUR KIDS THRIVE

concerns so you can authentically reflect the confidence you want to instill in them.

Children are incredibly adept at picking up on adult stress. If you feel overwhelmed due to work pressures, it's natural for your children to reflect that anxiety.

The science of "mirror neurons" supports this—these brain cells allow us to learn through observation.

Kids mimic behaviors they see, often reflecting our energetically triggered emotional states—this includes acting out when they're unsure how to voice discomfort with the energies they are feeling.

So, let's incorporate some more science:

Mirror Neurons

Have you heard of *mirror neurons*? These brain cells activate not only when we perform actions but also when we witness others doing so.

For instance, when someone smiles, our brain prompts us to smile back. This mirroring leads kids to learn by imitating—not through reasoning, but by observing our behaviors.

This mirroring mechanism plays a crucial role in social interaction and emotional understanding. When children observe the emotional expressions and behaviors of adults, their mirror neurons fire, allowing them to internalize and reflect those emotions.

Research has shown that mirror neurons help facilitate empathy, enabling children to grasp the emotions and intentions of others.

This is particularly important in their formative years, as children rely heavily on observation to learn how to navigate their social environments.

The energy that adults emit—whether it's stress, joy, or frustration—is not just seen but felt by children. They may mimic or even amplify these energies, acting out when they struggle to articulate their discomfort with what they perceive.

Moreover, this mirroring can manifest in behaviors such as biting when children feel anxious or overwhelmed by the attitudes, vibes, and tones that permeate their lives, whether directly or indirectly.

It's not a conscious choice;
rather, it is a reflection of their internal emotional state
and a response to the environment around them.

By understanding the role of mirror neurons, we can better appreciate the importance of vibing non-judgmental, peaceful emotional regulation, and mindful behavior. In doing so, we empower children to develop healthier ways to express their feelings.

With this foundation in mind, let's further explore the physical and energetic ramifications of mirroring on a young child's biting behavior.

Physical and Energetic Possibilities for Young Children's Biting

When it comes to biting behaviors in young children, there are two primary types of underlying reasons to consider: physical and energetic. It's essential to understand both as they contribute to a child's behavior.

1. Physical Reasons for Biting

Teething: One common physical reason for biting is teething. When young children's gums are sore and uncomfortable, they may resort to biting as a way to relieve that discomfort. It's always a good idea to have teething gel handy to help soothe their aching gums. Although less common, TMJD might be a reason.

2. Energetic Factors

In addition to physical factors, when children start biting for what appears to be "no good reason," it's important to remember that the person they bite is often mentally judgmental of them, which brings us to our next factor.

When addressing a child's behavior, the HAALTS method—Hungry, Angry, Anxious, Lonely, Tired, Screens—must always be the first consideration. This framework helps caregivers assess physiological and emotional needs that might lead to biting behavior.

- Holistic Assessment: By checking if a child is experiencing any HAALTS states, caregivers can address underlying issues before they escalate into biting. For example, a child who is tired may become irritable and more prone to biting when overstimulated.

- Energetic Interactions: Additionally, the HAALTS method delves deeper into the energetic interactions within the environment. Children are sensitive to the energetic and emotional states of those around them, which can significantly impact their behavior.

This is particularly true in light of the role of mirror neurons—children naturally mirror the energy, emotions, and behaviors of adults and peers. If an adult is stressed or angry, a child may pick up on this and reflect those feelings through biting or other disruptive behaviors.

Energetically Triggered Emotional Reactions

When young children bite seemingly without reason, it's often a mirroring reaction to the energetically triggering emotional state of the person they're with.

If that person is mentally judgmental or in a high state of dysregulation—experiencing rumination, fear, anger, anxiety, addiction, or depression—the child may feel overwhelmed by that energy or the absence of energetically available support that feeds their emotional well-being.

Judgmental vibes can lead them to act out in ways such as biting, as the atmospheric pressure of the emotional environment becomes unbearable for them, making the emotional climate around the child overwhelming.

Energetically Triggered Social Dynamics

A school principal in one of my online programs once shared her bafflement about a fourth grader biting other students in the hallways between classes for no apparent reason. No matter what they threatened the young boy with, he would not stop. My assignment for her that week was to observe him again, this time looking for what attitudes, vibes, or tones other students were giving him.

Upon observation, it became clear that the students he bit were taunting him, indicating that social dynamics may also drive biting behavior. This reflects the mirroring concept—just as children reflect the behaviors and emotions of adults, they also respond to their peers' dynamics.

Who should get a trip to the principal's office? Both, because it's time to get to the heart of the matter and resolve it between all who are involved, period.

Once again, this would be an excellent opportunity to use my *What, If, When Method* for facilitating conversations that get to the heart of the problematic behaviors on both sides of the conflict. To build a synergistic culture, it is imperative that we facilitate a constructive dialogue that encourages understanding and growth.

> Thoughts create energy, energy creates emotions, and emotions influence behavior, so it's vital to assess your emotional "temperature" before reacting.

By incorporating the HAALTS method—Hungry, Angry, Anxious, Lonely, Tired, Screens—and recognizing both physical and energetic factors, including the significant role of mirroring behaviors, caregivers can create a supportive environment for children, ultimately reducing the occurrence of biting behavior.

Time for a Vibe Check: Harnessing Our Energetic Influence

If you notice frustration over a minor issue, it can be that you are picking up on irritating vibes.

If this is happening to you, good news!

I've got 3 Energy Hacks for that coming up in Part II: Change Your Vibe.

Ultimately, being the adult in the room extends beyond behavior management; it's about recognizing that children often mirror our own emotional output.

As we navigate this journey, it's essential to embrace the messiness, learn from it, and foster nurturing connections.

By attuning our energy and adjusting our vibes, we create happier interactions and synergistic households, classrooms, and communities.

Picture your hectic day. Work pressures combine with kids' demands, and your internal dialogue is an energetic whirlwind—harsh, jarring, incongruous, or chaotic—of stress.

Kids absorb that energy and reflect it back in chaotic ways, such as meltdowns, because they can't verbalize their discomfort.

Feeling overwhelmed? It's time for a "temperature check." Look within before reacting; this is the golden rule! If you feel anxious, you might unintentionally create an unstable environment for your kids.

The silver lining? You can shift this energy! Do a *Quickie Vibe Check-In*. It's quick! Ready for you at: MaryReynolds.com/Gifts

Even on your busiest days, Stop-Look-Listen and you will automatically take a few deep breaths that will shift your energy and make a significant difference.

Sometimes You've Just Got to Drop Down and Cry

The pressures of adulthood can be overwhelming. There are times when your child's meltdown mirrors your own internal struggle, revealing just how heavy the weight of the world is on your shoulders. This can happen anywhere and everywhere. Two moments come to mind.

The first was when my son was almost three years old, and I was nearing the end of my savings. As a single mother with limited funds for groceries, I found myself in the checkout lane, stuck between two judgmental women whose disapproving looks and vibes only amplified my son's escalating frustration. He went into a full meltdown, and in that moment, I pulled him out of the cart, abandoned my groceries, and rushed us out to the car. I secured him in his car seat and hurried into the driver's seat. Unable to contain myself, I sat there and cried. He stopped. Then, I stopped. It was a soul-crushing experience—one that too many condescending individuals believe themselves entitled to impose on others.

The second moment occurred a few months later when I was not only starting a new full-time job but also teaching night classes while navigating a breakup with a man I thought I would marry. One evening, after a long day at work, my son collapsed onto the living room floor in a full meltdown. As I did my *Quickie Vibe Check-In*, I suddenly realized how incredibly sad and lonely I felt under the enormity of it all. I dropped to the floor beside him, and together we cried. Within 30 to 60 seconds, he sat up straight, looked at me with tears in his eyes, and said, "It's OK, Mommy."

Here's a Quick 3-Step Practice

Step 1: Visualize opening your arms wide and then gathering all that anxious energy back to yourself—a simple act that can transform your environment's ambiance from a battlefield to a nurturing space where everyone thrives.

Step 2: Put your hand on your heart and ask, "What's going on for me right now that I'm this upset?"

Step 3: From here, think about this: how you would prefer it to be? See where this answer takes you! Then follow your own advice and take actionable steps to get yourself there.

Something To Think About

Parenting goes beyond managing behaviors. It's essential to recognize that our children's actions often mirror our energetically infused emotional output. If they act out, pause to reflect on what may be happening within ourselves.

Educators, this principle applies to us as well—our energy and confidence about classroom management directly and indirectly influence student behavior. As we harness our energetic power, we foster peaceful interactions and create a supportive, synergistic environment.

By considering these energetic possibilities, caregivers and educators can better understand that biting and hitting behaviors, rather than being mere defiance, are expressions of missing skills, unmet needs, and overwhelming reactions to energetic influencers.

Ultimately, parenting, teaching, and leading are profound opportunities for self-discovery. By managing our energy, we can build supportive connections in both our families and classrooms. Embrace the chaos, learn from these reflections and find humor in the messiness.

As we move through this process together, remember that our kids are more than just mirrors; they are sensitive barometers of the energetically infused emotional climate. When we tune into our energy and adjust our vibes, we create healthier interactions and a more harmonious household, classrooms, and work places.

Next up, we'll break it down even further.

CHAPTER 13

SEEING WITH NEW EYES

In learning how to *See with New Eyes,* let's dive deeper into the profound impact of co-mingling, barometric pressure, and mirroring of emotional energy in homes, classrooms, and school cultures—all crucial elements that shape a child's behavior.

While toddlers hitting and biting can be alarming, these moments are just symptoms of deeper issues. They signal an energetic disconnect in their environment. Through personal anecdotes, like my experience with my son Brynie, it's time for us now to explore how children of all ages act as our emotional barometers, reflecting the underlying tensions around them.

Creating an energetically peaceful atmosphere begins with understanding and transforming the tone we set, whether at home or in school. By fostering open dialogue and employing strategies like my *What, If, When Method* (Part II), we can teach children the skill they are missing and the need to stand up and effectively advocate for themselves to grow into their own power.

Ultimately, the key is to acknowledge that children's behaviors are not intentional, deliberate disturbances; they're vital insights into the energetically infused emotional currents they navigate.

Let's embrace this knowledge to elevate our environments, enrich relationships, and nurture resilience in every child. It's time to shift our perspective and create a brighter future together! We start with toddlers.

Hitting, Biting Toddlers Continued

We're not done with this topic yet, as it is a major topic on social media.

A toddler hitting a parent isn't out of malice; it's a reflection of the energetically triggering emotional discomfort they're sensing. Hitting at the air in front of an adult's face or hitting their face is the child's reflexive reaction to "icky" energy. They are extremely uncomfortable with their care giver's vibes at that moment.

Quite often, it's a physical manifestation of their inability to articulate the overwhelming emotions and vibes surrounding them or flooding them.

When my son Brynie was two, I was dating a man I was considering marrying. He was an educator like me, so we had many interests in common. However, our parenting philosophies differed greatly. I focused on compassionate curiosity, social development, and collaboration, while he favored a more authoritarian approach that involved threats, isolation, and punishment to manage behavior.

I could feel that he had been containing his very harsh, skeptical, and judgmental attitude about my son, and then one evening when I was in the other room, Brynie bit him on the leg.

Because we weren't married yet, he told me he had refrained from doing what he had done with his own children and planned to do once we married—lock Brynie in a room and let him figure it out. Figure out what? Brynie was three!

Biting was unlike him; he was a sweet, well-behaved, loving little boy. This was the sign I needed. I had sensed something was off energetically, and needless to say, I did not marry him.

Instead of reacting with frustration, I approached the situation with compassionate curiosity. I turned to my *Quickie Vibe Check-List* to understand the behavior behind the biting. This moment revealed that when one adult harbors a judgment or negative attitude about a child, the child's reaction—like biting—spotlights the underlying tension.

Children may lack the words to express their feelings, but they can certainly sense the energetic atmosphere, shaping their behavior in ways we often overlook. Just as I did with Brynie, we need to pay attention to how our interactions impact our children.

Please Stop It Now!

Another *please stop it now* behavior can occur when you're engaged in a conversation with another adult that is energetically counterproductive, laced with indulgences like gossip and complaining, sending out waves of harmful, unnecessary negativity into the atmosphere.

Whenever I found myself in that kind of detrimental, possibly self-prophesizing self-indulgence, my son would start interrupting me, and he wouldn't stop until I stopped.

The next time your child or a student is excessively interrupting you, take a moment to reflect on what you're discussing or thinking about. This presents a valuable opportunity to consider the energy you are vibing.

Children are particularly sensitive—intuitive—to the energy around them, especially in situations filled with adult conflict, the influence of excessive alcohol, substance abuse, or financial stress.

The Tone of the Classroom

This phenomenon isn't restricted to just family dynamics; classrooms are equally affected. Teachers' energies can shape their students' learning experiences. An anxious or frustrated educator can inadvertently create an environment that is detrimental to both academic performance and emotional well-being.

When educators cultivate inclusive, synergistic, and open classroom environments characterized by welcoming atmospheres, it enhances learning and provides vital emotional support. A mind that feels welcome, wanted, and peaceful can think, learn, and thrive.

Now, I wouldn't be serving you well if I didn't let you know precisely how you can achieve this, regardless of the number of students you have or the concerns they may face. That's where my *9 Weeks to a Synergistic Classroom* curriculum comes in. It's designed to help you transform your classroom into a nurturing environment where every student can flourish.

The Tone of School Culture

Let's not overlook the broader school culture. Just as teachers can impact their classroom environment, school leaders set the tone for the entire institution. The collective energy—from administration to teachers to support staff—has a significant influence on the energetic safety and emotional well-being of students and staff.

A school culture infused with compassion, empowerment, skill development, and collaboration creates a ripple effect that fosters a supportive learning atmosphere and engenders growth. Conversely, environments steeped in fault-finding, complaining, victim mindsets, gossip, and mean-spiritedness can be detrimental.

If you have faculty members who habitually trade disparaging stories about various students and their parents in the waiting room outside the principal's office or in the teachers' lounge, that negativity can de-energize the entire school culture.

If this is a concern, I highly recommend doing a quick dive into my DFY: Done For You *9-Week's to a Synergistic Classroom* at: TeachingEnergetics.com/9WMDY

When Something Feels Off, It's Probably Off—Trust Yourself!

For parents who suspect something is off, don't delay—don't put your head in the sand. Get involved in your child's school and explore opportunities to collaborate with those in charge. Approach with curiosity and care, rather than fear and anger. Trust me when I say that this can be corrected.

To illustrate how school culture can dramatically affect a child's experience, let me share a personal story.

When my son Brynie was in 5th grade, he had a teacher who did not like him. He tried repeatedly to win her approval, prompting me to go in on more than one occasion to understand what was going on for her that made her so cruel to him.

After many attempts to collaborate with her, one day she went too far, excessively and unnecessarily humiliating him in front of the class. My son described both the teacher and her assistant as mean and awful.

Deeply concerned, I scheduled an appointment with the principal, who was in denial. She stated that this teacher was a twenty-five-year veteran with an unblemished reputation.

However, unblemished or not, neither she nor her supporting teacher were just hurting my son; they were actively emotionally crushing him. She firmly indicated that there would be no investigation into their behavior, so I asked for a transfer, making it clear that I was prepared to take the matter to the district if she didn't help remedy this situation.

The next day, when he was moved to a new classroom, the team of teachers to whom my son was assigned rolled their eyes at me during our first introductory meeting.

I'm not going to lie. It took everything I had to keep my vibes completely neutralized—peaceful—because being vibrationally hot with them for their blatant disregard and for minimizing the importance of this move would have set my son up for more of the same.

Teachers are tight-knit and protective of each other, and I understand that. If you are going to work with them, you must self-regulate at the highest level, which I discuss in depth in Part II: Change Your Vibe.

If you are a principal or school leader who must face these kinds of situations, you too must self-regulate your energy or be consumed by the turmoil that threatens to undermine your leadership.

     CHANGE YOUR VIBE, SEE YOUR KIDS THRIVE

It's not uncommon for those in leadership positions to struggle with the challenges posed by their faculty—especially those who gossip and speak out the most. Therefore, regulating energetically is essential, as is confronting issues non-confrontationally. We will be diving deeper into this approach in Part II.

Something To Think About

Have you ever walked into a school, house, office, or church and immediately felt like you had come home? Then you know exactly what I'm talking about.

Feeling welcomed and wanted is what we want today's children to experience each day as they walk through life's doors.

The bottom line: children act as our energy barometers, signaling when something is off. As the adult in the room, it is our responsibility to tune in, tap into our own vibes, and cultivate spaces where every single person feels seen, valued, and safe.

Today's children's behaviors are not merely disturbances; they are vital messages about the energetic and emotional landscape they navigate every day. By embracing this perspective, we can transform moments of chaos into opportunities for growth and deeper, energy-soothing connections, thereby creating an environment that nurtures everyone involved.

So the next time you're faced with a child's outburst or puzzling behavior, take a deep breath, pause, slow everything down, and consider what energetic currents might be at play.

By doing so, you not only empower yourself but also contribute to an empowering, synergistic environment that opens the door to profound healing and transformation for both you and the young lives you influence.

A Word About Consequences and Punishments

As we wrap up our approach to handling behaviors like hitting, biting, and throwing things, let's be clear: we don't hit children. Discipline isn't something a child discovers; it's a framework the adult installs. When we fail to respond firmly to aggressive behaviors, we're not teaching control; we're giving permission. Remember, children don't absorb discipline through the airwaves. They thrive on clear systems that hold firm, diffusing energetically laced emotional actions and reactions.

Think of discipline like bumper rails in a bowling alley—they're designed to bounce children back into productive behavior every single time. The goal isn't punishment; it's about creating an environment that supports learning and growth. When a chair is thrown, act without hesitation. Block the chair, remove distractions, hold and guide those hands down with calm assertiveness.

Structure precedes explanation; teaching comes after regulation. For example, if a child kicks, respond with firm, kind energy. Say, "I won't let you kick," while gently holding and guiding their hands downward. Remind them, "Feet are for standing, walking, and moving away." Reassure them, "We can talk when you're ready. For now, let's sit together and take a breather." (I prefer a breather to a time-out.)

In this approach, the energy you exude—firm, fair, and kind—makes all the difference. Consistency in your response will lead to cessation of big, scary behaviors. Remember, it's not about patience but about establishing clear protocols that prioritize energetic firmness while remaining kind. By putting these principles into practice, we can build a disciplined, nurturing environment where children flourish and meet their potential. Let's embrace our role in guiding them towards this brighter future.

CHAPTER 14

CHILDREN TEACH US WHAT WE NEED TO KNOW

As we delve into the next experiment in our exploration of the energetics of behavior, let's take a moment to reflect on a phenomenon that often goes unnoticed: the profound insights our children offer through their behavior.

Consider explosive and implosive behaviors as energetic display signs—similar to the dynamic speed feedback signs that inform drivers of their current speed, such as "YOUR SPEED IS." In this analogy, these signs would represent our energy levels, displayed as "YOUR ENERGY IS," guiding us as we strive to self-regulate during our interactions with children. Just as the signs help drivers adjust their speed, being aware of our energy can help us self-correct our energetic responses and create an environment that is supportive for children.

When a child acts out, they aren't just throwing a tantrum or appearing to be oppositional; they're sending us visual and auditory messages, urging us to adjust our approach and, let's be honest, perhaps even our own emotionally energized speed.

Imagine you're driving on a busy street, and you see that flashing speed sign—it's a nudge to slow down, take stock, and get back on course without getting defensive about it.

Have you ever noticed that sometimes your children's behavior seems to be reflecting the energy and attitude that you expect and project? It's dynamic, and it's something we often overlook.

Just as a driver self-corrects by adjusting their speed based on the information from these signs, we can use the feedback provided by children's behavior to gain insights into their emotional states and needs—whether they are feeling overwhelmed, excited, anxious, or insecure.

Our children serve as real-time indicators of how we might be inadvertently fueling their resistance, defiance, or what may appear to be disrespect. This correlation often boils down to our unique energetic atmosphere—comprised not only of our attitudes and vibes but also of the various tones we use in our daily interactions.

Children's behaviors may be signaling the need for a shift in the environment or a gentle recalibration of your own energy. Rather than reacting defensively, harshly, or dismissively, approach these moments with compassionate curiosity.

Ask yourself what might be influencing the child's emotional state. Look for external factors or examine your demeanor (use your free resource, *Quickie Vibe Check-List!*).

When children display erratic, explosive, or implosive behaviors, it's like they're saying, "Hey, something isn't right here! Can you dial down your judgmental attitudes, vibes, and tones until we can figure this out together?"

By tuning into the energetics of behavior, you open the door to transformative interactions, moving beyond merely managing the moment. Fully engaging with the energetic landscape fosters emotionally safe connections and deeper understanding.

The opportunity here isn't just about recognizing signs; it's about creating an atmosphere where children feel safe to express themselves. This ultimately leads to harmonious relationships and more meaningful communication.

Let's take a look at our next experiment.

Experiment #10: The Garden Grove School Zone Crackdown

Let's take a cue from the fascinating research reported in a *Wired Magazine* article, *The Mental Machine* by Thomas Getz—April 1995, Volume 3, Issue 4—which demonstrates that feedback loops heavily influence the human mind and subsequent behavior.

When children exhibit energetic discomfort or frustration, they're not just misbehaving; they're providing us invaluable feedback about the dynamics in play.

These moments demand our attention, offering an opportunity to reassess how we engage with them.

Are we judging, pressuring, or being impatient attitudinally?

Are we applying too much pressure? Are we moving too fast?

These are essential questions to consider.

Picture a child who is struggling in school and begins to shut down or act out. Instead of reacting with frustration, we can choose to interpret this behavior as a signal—a crucial opportunity to step back and recalibrate our energetically judgmental approach.

Rather than using our attitudes, vibes, and tones to convey our disappointment and then enforcing punitive rules, we can enjoy relationships built on mutual understanding and compassion.

At that moment, we transform from authority figures into collaborating partners in their development.

We've all heard stories of how communities have successfully tackled issues with innovative solutions.

Let's look at the Garden Grove experiment with dynamic YOUR SPEED IS displays, where authorities opted for an engaging way to prompt drivers to reconsider their speed without the fear of punishment.

If we opt to evaluate and modify our approach with children, we can help them correct their course without harsh judgments, focusing instead on understanding their energetically induced emotional landscape.

Are you getting this?

We can teach children, by our example, how to recognize their own energetic speed limits and self-correct without using intentionally hurtful attitudes, vibes, and tones when intervening on behaviors.

Let's remember, every time we encounter concerning behaviors, we have a choice.

Do we respond with energetic javelins of frustration, or do we turn inward and reflect on our own role in this feedback loop?

The latter approach not only enriches our relationships with our children but also nurtures their growth.

It's about creating an environment where they feel safe and understood, where they can learn to communicate their needs without fear.

By harnessing the energetic, non-judgmental power of the feedback loop, we can dramatically improve our ability to transform adult-child interactions.

So, the next time you find yourself facing a child's withdrawal or outburst, take a moment to pause for the cause.

Think of it as a YOUR ENERGY IS moment. You can self-correct right here, right now.

Recognize that you have the power to slow down, engage, and redirect your own energy in a constructive way that benefits everyone involved.

Beating yourself up and making yourself wrong is only more inflammatory energy—100% counterproductive. Just self-correct. Period.

You'll find that not only do their behaviors teach us valuable lessons, but they also pave the way for meaningful connections that can completely transform the dynamic.

In cultivating this mindset, we can unleash the untapped potential within our relationships with children.

They are teaching us what we truly need to know
—not just about the causes of their behaviors—
but about ourselves as well.

Let's *lean in* to these moments.

After all, when we adjust our "speed" to meet our children where they are energetically, we don't just guide them; we grow alongside them, fostering a rich, supportive environment that inspires everyone to thrive.

Something To Think About

As we connect all the dots throughout these last five chapters— Co-Mingling, Barometers and Mirroring, New Eyes, and Your Energy Is—it's crucial to acknowledge how our emotional energies influence our children's behavior and shape the overall environment we create at home and in the classroom.

The insights we've gained highlight the importance of understanding the interplay between our attitudes and the feelings children express. By recognizing our role in shaping this atmosphere, we can shift from reactions rooted in frustration to responses grounded in awareness and empathy.

But Wait! Before You Turn The Page

Now is the perfect time to get your next gift resource: my *Quickie Vibe Check-List*!

I'm excited for you to watch my 26-minute Micro-Dose resource video, complete with a beautiful full color 18" x 24" printable poster you can frame! The best part? You don't have to wait until you finish the book—this video complements this chapter perfectly. EnJoy!

Get your gifts! MaryReynolds.com/Gifts

PART II:
CHANGE YOUR VIBE

How to BE an HFT:

Human Frequency Transformer

CHAPTER 15

VIBES OVER VERBIAGE HOW YOUR ENERGY SHAPES RELATIONSHIPS

Welcome to Part II: Change Your Vibe

When normal parenting, teaching, and discipline feels impossible.

When kids implode or explode or turn violent for no apparent reason.

When you're anxious about your kid at home or kids in your school.

> Changing your vibe is simple compared to
> remembering pages and pages of scripts and phrases
> in the heat of the moment—especially
> when disciplining feels impossible!

By now, you are realizing that the adult in the room has all the energetic power to either blow things up or soothe things down through attitudes, vibes, and tones.

While physical connection is a significant percentage of what every child needs, non-judgmental, energetic connection is the cornerstone for everything coming before, during, and after an upsetting situation.

The big idea here is that there are energetic components to the transformative power of connection. It's not just about you being in the room, making better attempts at connecting by having more one-on-one time, using affirmative language and positive reinforcement.

And while people are using these techniques properly, they don't know why they're still not getting better, self-sustaining results with some kids.

Now, I'm just going to say it here. If this is you, the main reason you are not getting better results is likely that it is you who must be the one to change the energetics of your attitudes, vibes, and tones in order to connect with the "problematic" individuals who are not responding as you would like them to. The energetics must be congruent with the message to sync up communication.

For example, if you really don't like a child, student, or even a colleague, there's an invisible energetic chasm that all the words of encouragement in the world will not make your life easier with them.

Vibes Don't Lie

I know what you may be thinking, "But Mary, this kid has done this thing that he's been told not to do for the umpteenth time and now I am on my last nerve. The last thing I can do in that moment is to change my vibe when I can't even calm myself down."

I understand that, before today, this has been how it plays out despite your best efforts, but play along with me here.

What if you are ready to lose it all on this kid, when out of the blue, the most compassionate, affirmative, non-judgmental person you know walks through the door. You'd very likely be able to change your vibe in an instant.

Change Your Vibe

If you stop for just 30 seconds and think about how you are connecting energetically—attitudes, vibes, and tones—you will be able to quickly put an end to so many upsetting, time-consuming situations.

Now don't overthink this.

It's not about perfection; it's about practicing to build muscle memory, and about the progress that can come from changing your vibration.

Changing your vibe is not telling yourself to calm down.

Changing your vibe is about suspending all judgment in the moment.

There are a lot of different ways to *Change Your Vibe* quickly.

It can be as simple as smiling.

Loving instead of judging.

Having compassionate curiosity instead of coming down hard.

Relabeling a kid in your mind, and practicing selective amnesia as an antidote to others' life-limiting labels.

Energy Hacking Behavior: Transforming Every Size of Upset

In today's fast-paced world, we often witness explosive and implosive behaviors in children—responses that stem from overwhelming emotions in energetically chaotic environments.

These behaviors can be distressing not just for the children themselves but also for parents, teachers, and caregivers who strive to create calm, nurturing spaces.

But what if I told you that the key to transforming these upsetting dynamics lies within the energy that flows among us?

By harnessing the power of Energy Hacking, we can effectively interrupt, redirect, and transform these behaviors into constructive expressions of growth and understanding.

Energy Hacking is about becoming aware of and actively managing the energetic exchanges that occur in our interactions with children.

Just as a skilled musician knows how to adjust their instrument to create harmony, we too can learn to navigate the energetically triggered emotional landscape that surrounds us.

We can build the mental muscle for this.

When a child exhibits volatile behaviors or shuts down emotionally, it is often a response to the energy they've absorbed from their environment, be it positive or negative.

I've created several short videos for you to illustrate even further how our energies infuse the children in our care: MaryReynolds.com/Videos

By implementing intentional Energy Hacks, we can shift the atmosphere, empower our children to self-regulate, and create a foundation for constructive communication.

Are you ready? I am excited to share my top 3 Energy Hacks designed to interrupt destructive patterns and foster resilience in our children.

These hacks are not just tools; they are transformative practices that encourage children and adults to recognize their energy, emotions, embrace their feelings, and express themselves in healthier ways.

Through understanding the connection between energy, behavior, and emotional self- and co-regulation, we can create environments that not only mitigate explosive and implosive reactions but also cultivate deeper emotional intelligence.

Join me as we explore these impactful hacks and empower ourselves to become catalysts for change in our children's lives!

If you're ready to transform your emotional atmosphere from chaos to serenity, buckle up!

It's time to dive into my top three hacks that will elevate your vibe and inspire those around you. Together, we can foster meaningful connections and strengthen our relationships.

CHAPTER 16

MY #1 GO-TO ENERGY HACK

TurnAround Big Explosive and Implosive Behaviors in 30 Seconds

More often than not, over the past four decades, I've turned around big scary behaviors, in 30 seconds or less, by navigating the ever-shifting currents of human behavior energetically. Through all the complexities and opportunities, I've distilled my approach to just three fundamental Energy Hacks.

No matter the situation—whether you're grappling with explosive defiance from a child or navigating the more subtle yet equally distressing implosive behaviors in both children and adults, these strategies have proven to be my unwavering go-tos.

Each one offers a straightforward approach to energetically diffuse outwardly disruptive actions while also addressing the quiet withdrawal and frustration that can arise in more indirect interactions. Together, these 3 Energy Hacks will empower you to create impactful shifts in any emotional landscape!

Don't dismiss their simplicity or ease of application.

You see, there's absolutely no need to complicate the energetics of any scenario. When you strip away the layers of confusion and focus on these three hacks, you'll find yourself equipped to handle just about anything that comes your way.

Think of them as your energetic toolkit for transformation.

Reflect for a moment: Have you ever felt overwhelmed by a child's outburst or a difficult interaction? You're not alone. Keep these hacks in mind, and you'll be golden!

Energy Hack #1: High Vibe It!—Suspend Judgment

Get yourself immediately into an AFZ: Attitude Free Zone.

How do you do that?

Easy.

SUSPEND ALL JUDGMENT right here, right now. You can revisit your judgments later if you feel it's necessary. However, if you still want to diffuse an explosive situation energetically, you must stop labeling it as right or wrong, good or bad—despite how it may initially *appear*.

Such labeling is what creates the *illusion* of behavior; it's often not what it seems until you dive deeper and change your vibe, which is where the real *magic* lies.

As the adult in the room, you have all the power to influence what happens next by what you energetically interject into the situation with your attitudes, vibes, and tones.

The instant you suspend all judgment, *your* energy changes for the better.

When your energy changes, your soothing—zero content—vibe will energetically neutralize the likelihood of the person erupting or stone-walling.

The number one mistake I see so many adults make is launching attitudinal and verbal judgments with uninformed assessments made in the moment, without ever asking "what's" going on for the person involved. The key realization is that:

You cannot judge and love in the same moment.

The moment you feel justified in criticizing another's "bad" actions, you intensify conflict. Instead, shift your focus to your own energy. To transform the energetics of an undesirable situation, you must first decide that you are going to manage your impulse to:

abandon

avoid

diminish or

punish

... to make your point or control behavior.

The very best place to begin is

Behavior Modification's #1 Rule:

Before you can change anyone else,

you must first change yourself!

We bravely start with ourselves. What we honestly think about a child or adult has everything to do with our vibes.

Vibes Don't Lie

If you don't like a child, or perceive that child as "the enemy," you will be unable to work effectively with them.

You are either contaminating or contributing based on what you've decided about any given situation.

Your perceptions regarding a person profoundly affect your energy. If you don't resonate and align with a child or adult, effective collaboration becomes nearly impossible. Your attitude is never secret; it emits energy into your environment.

Those who habitually default to punitive actions—like humiliation, punishment, seclusion, exclusion, expulsion, and abandonment—believe that hurting individuals teaches lessons. However, these methods rarely yield mentally healthy, sustainable results. As James Lehman, MSW, author of *Transform Your Child*, emphasizes, "There is no excuse for abuse."

While some claim they turned out fine despite enduring similar tactics, we must aim for more than just "fine." Why not strive for thriving?

My *High Vibe It* Energy Hack is validated by the works of Dr. David Hawkins, who introduced the *Map of Consciousness* in *Power vs. Force*. This model connects emotional states to vibrational frequencies.

Higher frequencies, linked to love, joy, and peace, can dissolve negativity, making these responses powerful tools in transforming difficulties. In other words, higher vibes can diffuse lower vibes. The *Map of Consciousness* ranges from low-vibrational states like shame and fear to high-vibrational states like love and enlightenment.

Lower levels, which include shame and guilt, diminish personal empowerment, while the higher levels foster connection and growth.

Here's a summary of some key levels from Hawkins' *Map of Consciousness* as it relates to my *High Vibe It* Energy Hack.

LOW VIBING IT—Weakest State: 1. Shame (20) 2. Guilt (30) 3. Apathy (50) 4. Grief (75) 5. Fear (100) 6. Desire (125) 7. Anger (150) 8. Pride (175)

MEDIUM VIBING IT: 9. Courage (200) 10. Neutrality (250) 11. Willingness (310) 12. Acceptance (350) 13. Reason (400)

HIGH VIBING IT—Strongest State: 14. Love (500) 15. Joy (540) 16. Peace (600) 17. Enlightenment (700–1000)

Here's what is so important about this:

Each vibrational level is associated with specific emotional states and attitudes, and as you move up the scale, there is an increase in strengthening (soothing and empowering) qualities and a decrease in weakening (inflammatory and irritating) ones.

For example, levels like (unconditional, agape) love, joy, and peace represent higher states of consciousness that result in increased personal empowerment and connectedness.

This scale is not intended to be a rigid structure but rather a tool for self-awareness and personal development. It's important to note that the numbers represent a logarithmic relationship, meaning that **lower levels hold significantly less power than higher ones**.

Instead of coming down hard on problematic behavior, learn a better way to confront non-confrontationally, which I'm going to tell you about in the next Energy Hack.

For now, something to think about is that *High Vibing It* can be as simple as thinking of someone and sending them your love, or when you are really upset, start a mental mantra: peace, joy, love, and light—peace, joy, love, and light—peace, joy, love, and light. Or you can even do a mental meditative Ohm—Ohm—Ohm—Ohm—Ohm—Ohm.

It's like flipping on a light switch in a dark room; suddenly, everything appears lighter, more manageable.

The second thing that happens is that, when you focus your mind on peace, joy, love, and light, you will automatically take a deep breath. This action activates your brain, turning the light back on in your frontal lobe and allowing ideas to emerge, which can help you move the situation toward a peaceful resolution and restoration.

When you activate this simple Energy Hack, you're not just reacting—you're intentionally creating non-judgmental, peaceful vibes in your mind first, which next infuses the energetic environment. Things can improve quickly.

It feels like a miracle!

This will give you a great start to turning around situations in your life that, before now, have been de-energizing, if not seemingly impossible to improve.

But there's more!

When I first started writing this book, my intention was to fully explore *The Miracle Regulator* in this chapter because it is central to *High Vibing It*.

However, as I outlined it, I realized that it deserves to be a stand-alone book in its own right and is now included in *The Miracle Regulator* Micro-Dose resource, which is mentioned many times throughout this book because it fast-tracks better results.

It's been said that a picture is worth a thousand words and a video is worth ten thousand—meaning that a video can communicate even more complex narratives and emotions.

So, rather than trying to incorporate it into this book, I've created a resource video for you.

The Miracle Regulator is something you truly have to see to fully understand the energetics at play in real time, which affect us all day, every day.

The challenges we face stem not only from our thoughts but also from how those thoughts can make us more receptive or de-energized in our everyday situations and interactions with others.

As an extension of my *High Vibe It* Energy Hack, I encourage you to explore my *Miracle Self-and Co-Regulator* video.

In it, I share not only the ONE thing you can do when you don't know what to do but also my journey of discovering this as my #1 Go-To no matter what.

The number one request I get from my audiences is people just wanting shortcuts to stop anger and violence quickly. Even though they're using all of the prescribed techniques.

The most significant concerns coming in are about kids diagnosed with EBD—Emotional and Behavioral Disordered—with violent tendencies.

While addressing their hurts and internal pain is an ongoing concern for kids with this diagnosis, what people need is a way to stop it in its tracks.

Other than room clears—or locking their kid in a room where they can't hurt you or others in the family and scream for hours—what can be done?

So, the question is: "Will the Miracle Regulator stop meltdowns, tantrums, and even violent situations?" As with anything in life, it depends on the situation and everything leading up to it.

Let me preface this by saying there are two scenarios to consider:

> First, when a child is being violent, the primary concern will always be about safety: yours, theirs, and anyone nearby. Use the recommended tools you have already invested in or are required to learn. If you need to run, then run.

> Second, if there is no place for you to run, like on an airplane, then what I'm going to show you in the *Miracle Self- and Co-Regulator* has the potential to influence you and create coherence with those near to you in an energetically soothing way, which can and has literally saved lives.

Hopefully, you will not be able to unsee what I'm going to illustrate for you in my Micro-Dose resource video.

MiracleRegulator.com

This brings us to my second Energy Hack, which is to energetically connect with compassion first, using my *What, If, When Method*.

TWO MORE ENERGY HACKS

Behavioral Improvement at Lightning Speed!

As we continue in our journey, it's essential to remember the profound impact of our choices in how we engage energetically with one another. We now delve into the next two critical Energy Hacks, which can revolutionize the way we navigate relationships: compassion and the power of language.

Energy Hack #2: What, If, When It—Put Compassion First!

You might be skeptical about compassion, fearing it could lead to manipulation by children. But trust me, compassion is not a weakness; it's a transformative energy that can heal and uplift both you and those around you.

If you're curious about the profound impact of compassion, I invite you to explore my resource, *The Power of Compassion: 7 Ways You Can Make A Difference*, which includes the inspiring Teddy Stallard Story. You can access it at: MakeADifference.com as an additional thank you for interest in this book.

The energetics of compassion acts as both a self-regulating tool and a way to co-regulate—generate coherence—with others. Unlike empathy, which taps into someone's pain, compassionate energy creates a safe space for them to explore and express their struggles.

The key to understanding this dynamic? One powerful, simple open-ended question:

"What's going on for you that_____?"

This shifts the energy and allows for deeper understanding.

I know what you may be thinking—there are kids you can barely tolerate, making it hard to muster even an ounce of compassion. I've been there! Yet, my commitment to using the *What, If, When It Energy Hack* has proven effective time and again, even when it feels impossible.

Start with compassion by asking "what" rather than "why." This simple shift fosters a head-to-heart connection, especially with kids and adults who struggle to express themselves effectively. It stops excuse making once and for all.

Compassion changes the dynamic, transforming "Me" into "We," which is essential for collaboration and understanding.

Using compassion means you're less likely to resort to unnecessary or even extreme punishments that can exacerbate issues further. Quick mental and emotional shifts can yield miraculous results in just about 30 seconds, especially with children exhibiting explosive or defiant behaviors.

Research from the Gottman Institute observes that:

Compassion leads to favorable outcomes 70% of the time. Resentment guarantees failure results 100% of the time.

Moreover, Steven Stosny's *Compassion Power* program reveals that compassionate thoughts "light up" the brain's frontal lobe, activating cognitive functions like problem-solving.

In contrast, resentment dims that light, leading to shut down and dysfunction. So, compassionate energy not only improves relationships but also promotes healthier mental processes.

I've applied this technique in my second marriage and found great success. For instance, one day, my husband's distracting antics during my football pregame show pushed me right to the edge of my last nerve. Instead of responding with my usual frustration, I used my *What, If, When It* Energy Hack and asked, "What's going on for you that you're doing that thing that I've asked you not to do?"

His initial response was, "I don't know." When I added, "If you did know what might it be?" He still didn't know. I ended with, "When you do know, I really want to know. It matters to me. For now, let's watch the game." It wasn't long before he was able to reach for the "heart" of it. He discovered that he had been feeling excluded, just as he had been as a child. This profoundly simple insight resolved our misunderstanding and transformed our communication.

If you are prepared to approach behavior differently, my *What, If, When It* Energy Hack is quick and effective. Expect better results in 30 seconds or less more often than not. This method empowers individuals, allowing you to defuse contentious situations easily.

Consider using it whenever you observe harmful behavior, gently addressing the root cause. Ask, "What's happening that led you to do or say that?" If they're unsure, guide them with: "If you did know, what would it be?" Then, if they still don't know, assure them, "When you do know, I want you to let me know. Let's put a pin in it for now and get back to what we were doing."

This technique transforms unproductive behaviors and makes individuals feel valued. Consider Martha's experience in her own words, using my *What, If, When It* Energy Hack with a habitually distressed foster child whose explosions could last for thirty minutes or more.

"I used your *What, If, When It* Energy Hack with a twelve-year-old who was screaming, ranting, raving, and hitting himself because he was very angry about something, though I wasn't sure what it was. There was just a lot of activity and yelling. So, I asked him the 'What' question, and, of course, I looked around to see if something else needed to happen, like if he was in trouble or danger. But when I asked him that question, he just said (as you predicted), 'I don't know.'

"So, I moved to the next line and asked him, 'If you did know, what might it be?' He kept yelling, but within less than a minute his anger and energized frustration dropped from about a 10 out of 10 to around a 9 or an 8.

"In the past, I would have tried to fix it, solve it, or reassure him that everything would be fine, but instead of trying to solve it—which never seemed to work—I stayed with this line of questioning and waited.

"Eventually, he opened up and told me why he was upset and what was going on. It turned out to be an issue I never would have guessed: he was talking about how he hates change and all the details surrounding that. By being present and as peaceful as possible while listening, I found that the entire conversation lasted only about four to five minutes.

"It ended with him almost falling asleep because he had the opportunity to express what was really going on for him. I found this approach very helpful; it allowed him to express himself without me trying to solve it for him or fix it. I had good success with that assignment."

Miraculous! With her peaceful, compassionate *What, If, When It* questioning, Martha facilitated a breakthrough in less than a couple of minutes that calmed him significantly, leading to a productive outcome. She learned something she would have never thought of without his input.

I wanted to share another mind-blowing success story from Dona, an Educational Administrator in Ohio in her own words:

"I had several opportunities to use the technique this week, and I tried it multiple times. I want to share one particularly impactful situation I had today with a 16-year-old student. As an administrator at a charter school, I often encounter students who come for various reasons.

"In this instance, another administrator was with the student, who was becoming increasingly upset and raising his voice. I stepped in and calmly asked, 'What is it that you're so upset about right now?' The student responded multiple times with 'I don't know.'

"So, I followed up with, 'If you did know, what would it be?' This approach worked to help him calm down and reflect. As we talked, the situation revealed deeper issues; he eventually expressed that he was really upset with his mom.

"This response highlighted the complexity of his feelings, which we've known about for a while. After our conversation, I was able to have him in a quiet space where he could focus better and actually complete some work, which has been challenging for him in the past.

"Throughout this week, I found that my peaceful demeanor and this technique consistently helped others reflect and respond thoughtfully, which has been eye-opening for me. I've also noticed others beginning to adopt this approach after seeing me model it, which is encouraging!

"Overall, it was a very productive week, and I'm eager to continue exploring this technique."

I've witnessed countless seemingly miraculous results, and you can too. If you're ready for a new approach, let's foster compassion and expand our potential to create harmony in our environments.

By embracing compassion, we aren't just helping ourselves; we're enhancing the collective well-being around us.

Let's harness this dynamic force and elevate every aspect of our lives! To dive deeper and learn the nuances of this method, check out my *What, If, When Method: How to Confront Non-Confrontationally* Micro-Dose resource video at: WhatIfWhenMethod.com

Energy Hack #3: ReLabel It - Unlocking Problematic Behaviors

Have you ever thought about the energetic impact of labels?

When a label is repeatedly applied to someone with emotion and energy, it becomes a pocket of vibrational frequency that the psyche absorbs. This brings us to *ReLabel It*!

Relabeling is crucial for reversing unproductive behaviors. By changing life-limiting labels, you can start altering not just behaviors, but also the learning capabilities of the labeled individuals.

Consider whether these are the stories you want to nurture. Often, life-limiting labels are carelessly applied, and unfortunately, they prevent us from achieving constructive interactions.

You might wonder how to relabel problematic behaviors you encounter daily. The answer lies in changing your mindset; when you shift your energy, you open the door to new possibilities.

Remember, energy flows where attention goes. If you focus on fostering productive behavior, that's where the energy will go.

For example, if a child is labeled as "manipulative," what's actually happening is often missed. The child is merely trying to have their needs acknowledged in the ways that they have learned.

Instead of criticizing this behavior as wrong, relabel it as "self-advocating," which describes what they are genuinely trying to ask for. When you revise your attitude about a child's behavior, you greatly increase the chances of avoiding unnecessary power struggles.

This shift in vibe helps prevent the child from feeling like they have to become your enemy in order to be heard.

I once worked with a family who believed their four-year-old daughter was "controlling" and "manipulative." After discussing her behavior in light of her developmental stage, we relabeled her as a "self-advocating girl." Almost immediately, their communication and relationship improved.

Yet, as Eric Jensen explains in *Teaching with the Brain in Mind*, children are not solely defined by their DNA; rather, their genomes are activated and shaped by their experiences. Epigenetics demonstrates that environmental factors, including our interactions and experiences, can influence gene expression beyond just the genetic code we inherit.

For instance, the language we use—life-limiting labels—can impact gene expression related to emotional stress, highlighting the profound connection between our words and the biological processes within us.

Contrary to common beliefs, changing an adult's attitude can make a significant energetic impact on children with serious emotional and behavioral challenges.

Many behavioral programs fail because they rely on rewards and punishments—extrinsic versus intrinsic motivation—without considering the energetic factors that precede behavior. As I've stated before, rewards and punishments ignore the energetics at play.

The Other Elephant in the Room: Acronym-ademic!

We have become a society that excessively overreacts, over-problematizes, overcomplicates, overanalyzes, overdiagnoses, and overmedicates—all of which contribute to a heightened sense of anxiety.

Let's address the rapid increase of acronyms for disorders—what I term as "Acronym-ademic" or "Acronym-mania." In 2016, there were 26 acronyms for behavioral disorders; now, there are 45.

Even more alarming is that far too many children are being diagnosed with 2 to 5 disorders, leading to them being labeled

"Alphabet Soup Kids." This explosion of acronyms might seem like progress, but it increases the risk of self-fulfilling prophecies that may hinder growth.

Now let's shake things up even more, because I am not the only one drawing attention to excessive life-limiting labeling. In light of this perspective, it's crucial to consider the implications of traditional diagnostic labeling.

Experts Warn There's a Huge Problem With Diagnostic Labeling

According to an explosive study in the *Journal of Psychiatry Research,* the authors conclude that diagnostic labeling—making psychiatric diagnoses based solely on symptom clusters—is scientifically meaningless and disingenuous.

> Lead researcher Dr. Kate Allsopp from the University of Liverpool stated, "Although diagnostic labels create the illusion of an explanation, they are scientifically meaningless and can create stigma and prejudice."
>
> This research underscores the importance of our approach: instead of confining individuals to limiting labels, we should focus on understanding the underlying issues—such as trauma and other adverse life experiences—that contribute to the behaviors being assessed. By moving beyond diagnoses, we can foster an environment that emphasizes potential, healing, and growth.
>
> Professor Peter Kinderman, University of Liverpool, said: "This study provides yet more evidence that the biomedical diagnostic approach in psychiatry is not fit for purpose. Diagnoses frequently and uncritically reported as 'real illnesses' are in fact made on the basis of internally inconsistent, confused

and contradictory patterns of largely arbitrary criteria. The diagnostic system wrongly assumes that all distress results from disorder and relies heavily on subjective judgments about what is normal."

Professor John Read, University of East London, said: "Perhaps it is time we stopped pretending that medical-sounding labels contribute anything to our understanding of the complex causes of human distress or of what kind of help we need when distressed."

This study highlights the critical need to reconsider our reliance on diagnostic labels. As these experts assert, the labels often obscure rather than clarify the complexities of human behavior and distress.

The increase in life-limiting diagnosing and labeling can lead to overanalysis paralysis, blinding us to holistic solutions.

Not only is a medical-sounding label unhelpful because symptoms and treatment options are so diverse, it can also cause unnecessary hardship for many who then live their lives according to their "label," which often deprives them of the help they could benefit from.

While getting a "diagnosis" is often necessary to access financial and physical resources for helping our children, it may weaken the resolve to intercede energetically where opportunities to heal exist for today's children and ourselves.

Conversely, affirmative labels can empower, not limit. Change begins by relabeling. For instance, instead of viewing a child as having "ADHD," think of them as "creative" or "kinesthetic." If you can just think this one thing, your vibe will infuse them with a higher level belief and expectation that they can learn, focus, and be productive.

Several years ago, I received a Facebook message from a former student who was dyslexic saying, "Because you believed I could, I did." She graduated from high school and is living a beautiful prosperous life.

If you find it impossible to believe that many disorders can be healed, I invite you to explore the story of Raun K. Kaufman, an expert who has fully recovered from autism. His experiences are detailed in *Autism Breakthrough: The Groundbreaking Method.*

Here's an exercise to facilitate this transformation:

Step 1: Write down all the negative labels you hold (your vibe) for a child who frustrates you. Assess your energy on a scale of 1-10.

Step 2: Create a corresponding affirming label (new vibe) for each negatively limiting one. Reassess your energy afterward.

Step 3: Reflect on any self-imposed limiting beliefs. Shift your language and mindset to these new labels and feel the difference in your energy toward this child.

Something To Think About

> Relabeling is not about denying reality;
> it's about planting seeds for positive growth.

Our family adopted a traumatized shelter dog named Angel, who was both fearful and aggressive.

By relabeling her as my "sweet girl," and visualizing her success, we transformed her behavior over time with consistency.

Beginning with the end in mind, I envisioned getting her to a place where I could safely walk with her unleashed. My goal was achieved with affirmative languaging, "my sweet, sweet girl," along with consistent skill development and the corresponding vibration of our expectation. Dogs are as tuned into vibes as children are.

I want you to unleash the potential in your students or children.

Remember, no matter what their diagnoses or concerns, you can influence profound change. Through a willingness to learn how to navigate energy, you can raise your attitudes, vibes, and tones.

By applying these 3 Energy Hacks, you can easily transform your environment and foster growth.

For more insights, check out my Micro-Dose resource videos: *No Labels, No Limits: How to Unlock Problematic Behaviors*, found at: NoLabelsNoLimits.com

In the next chapter, "Infinitesimal Vibes," we will delve deeper into the subtle energies that might go unnoticed yet significantly impact our interactions with students like Brandon.

His story exemplifies how even the most minor shifts in energy can lead to profound changes in behavior, emotional connection, and academic acceleration.

Prepare to uncover the layers of influence that shape student experiences, and learn how to quickly harness these infinitesimal vibes, transforming how you engage with the children in your life.

Together, we'll unlock the power of awareness and intentionality as we continue this transformational journey.

CHAPTER 18

INFINITESIMAL VIBES

As I've alluded to in the introduction to this book, I had prided myself on using my special "Magic" to help all my students be successful in their classwork. But one year, I had a student who wouldn't do his work. No amount of encouragement helped; Brandon wasn't coming through. After many months of doing everything I could —what I believed were the "right" things to do with him—I became quite agitated.

The inner dialogue I experienced one day sounded like this:

> "How dare he not respond to me. I'm an awesome teacher. Doesn't he know how lucky he was to make it into my classroom? All the kids in the school want to be in my classroom. What an ungrateful little boy he is!"

Whether we realize it or not, we all have negative attitudes about some of the people we love, live with, or work alongside. No matter how slight it may seem, that attitude is amplified, loud and clear.

As I've said before, the end result is the equivalent to yelling, "Get up!" at someone while simultaneously pushing them down to the ground with your foot on their shoulder, holding them there. Once again, I must reiterate:

These insidious bonds we have with one another are energetically destructive to both parties involved. It de-energizes us to hold a negative charge because it produces results that frustrate us. And our negative energy directed at others also has a neurophysiological effect on them, as we continue to send it. (Learn more about the Catch-22 of life-limiting labels found in my Micro-Dose resource videos, *No Labels, No Limits* at: NoLabelsNoLimits.com)

Coming to this realization, it is not about beating ourselves up or considering ourselves in the wrong for the attitudes we presently hold. It is essential to be willing to make different decisions in recognizing the gifts, talents, and offerings we are intended to bring to this world, as well as those of the children whose lives we are trying to impact.

Our work on attitudes about the people we are having difficulty with is never really complete. However, it does become easier to be honest with ourselves about what we've been believing and holding at the deepest parts of ourselves.

We can't go back and undo what's been done energetically but sending good vibes can heal and transform adult-child interactions.

Changing the Trajectory of Brandon's Life

By the time Brandon was assigned to my classroom, I had gained a great deal of knowledge about the energetics of attitudes and expectations. For many years, since I took the Behavior Modification class in my master's degree program, I had been practicing the #1 Rule in all my dealings with people:

Before you can change anyone else,
you must first change yourself.

I endeavored deliberately not to hold an attitude about the children who came into my classes with histories of problematic behavior or who had been labeled as "underachievers."

That night, after I went home, I sat quietly at the kitchen table, pondering my thoughts about Brandon. Because this #1 Rule was always at the forefront of my mind, and because I was used to shifting my attitude, I had been able to bring all the other children I worked with to very high levels of success and self-esteem. But nothing was working with Brandon. How could that be?

My 30-Second TurnAround

I sat there and thought, "Before I can change anyone else, I must first change myself. But what is it that I need to change?"

It was in the quiet of that moment that I was able to find the most profound thought I had buried in the recesses of my mind. It was a thought that directly affected the energy my attitude was inadvertently transmitting to Brandon, and I had completely missed it.

It seemed irrelevant, so small a thought, so infinitesimal, that I could barely believe it was even there.

But it was there, and it wasn't so small after all. Once I recognized it, the thought was so big and loud that it was deafening. When I looked at Brandon, I saw a kid whose parents were alcoholics and drifters. The teachers all believed that Brandon would probably not be with us for long, as his parents frequently changed jobs and moved from one place to another.

I knew, down to my toes, that the #1 Rule always worked when I worked it, but I never guessed that I would discover such a terrible bias buried deep inside of me.

I cried a deep and soulful cry for a while, unburdening my heart. I was so shocked by my prejudice. I had no idea I held a bias about people from "the wrong side of the tracks!" Where did that come from? I had no idea.

After I recovered, I decided not to beat myself up for this; I just acknowledged it and owned responsibility for how pivotal it had been in denying me the ability to teach Brandon anything.

You Can't Have an Attitude and Keep It A Secret!

The next day, when I approached Brandon and worked with him on his lessons, my heart felt free, and my attitude was warm, welcoming, and reasonably expectant. I did not tell him about my revelation. I did not lecture him again. I did not do any rah-rah stuff for him. I was simply energetically different with him. My energy was intentional and on purpose.

I didn't know if it would make any difference, but lo and behold, he began participating at a higher level almost immediately and gained self-confidence quickly.

The proof is in the results, and Brandon showed me that my "new bias-free attitude" was what he needed to perform up to his capabilities. To my delight, and his as well, his grades improved from Ds to Cs and Bs in the subsequent weeks.

His parents did move on, but my last memory of Brandon was the light in his eyes and the smile on his face. It was then, and only then, that I could say I had done my best to be of service.

Let's continue ...

CHAPTER 19

THE ENERGETIC POWER OF EXPECTATION

An expectation is simply an extension of our underlying attitude, and the step from one to another is a short one. It is something that we have all been able to sense coming from others, whether they mean to convey it or not. We all know who believes in us and who doesn't.

For example, if we consider a child "less than" capable of learning, we automatically form very low expectations of their chances of attending college. When the student later drops out of high school, convinced he's a loser, it's no surprise to us. This silent, yet energetically pervasive, expectation is known as "a self-fulfilling prophecy."

While the cause-and-effect relationship between attitudes or expectations and results can sometimes be elusive to trace in adult interactions, it is relatively easy to observe in children.

Its elusiveness may be because kids are more of a "clean slate"—they have not yet formed the deep-seated habits and belief systems that adults typically have. Additionally, children's lives are relatively simple compared to the complex and stressful lives most adults lead, so the effects of our inputs are more discernible.

In the energetic balance between individuals, the person who holds the strongest belief about a situation will almost always prevail. In this respect, adult expectations usually prevail over the outcomes children can produce. This next experiment, a study on the expectations of teachers, is an excellent example:

Teachers' Expectations Carried Out by Students
in a Profound Way

Experiment #11: The Pygmalion Effect

When it comes to learning, the expectations that teachers hold can profoundly shape student outcomes. The Pygmalion Effect, a fascinating psychological phenomenon, was explored by researchers Robert Rosenthal and Lenore Jacobson (1964) in a groundbreaking experiment at an elementary school in California.

They aimed to investigate the impact of teacher expectations on student performance, using accepted experimental controls.

The researchers used a standard IQ test to grade all the students. The teachers were all told that this was a "new" test, which measured "bloomers," predicting rapid academic advancement, regardless of their past academic achievements. Furthermore, they were given a list of 20 randomly selected students who were expected to be "bloomers."

At the end of the school year, the same IQ test revealed that the 20 students randomly tagged as "bloomers" had made significantly more academic progress than the students not on the list, some more than twice as much.

The teachers were amazed and wanted to know the secret of how this new test identified these extraordinary students. When the teachers learned that they had been given a random list of students, they themselves expressed their realization that their thoughts and expectations truly matter, reinforcing Rosenthal and Jacobson's suggestion that high expectations influence student outcomes.

An important aspect of this and over 500 similar studies is that the students were never informed of the "labels" they were given, and no students were ever told that they were inferior. In the real world, we make our beliefs about children known to them, in a variety of ways. Even when not explicitly expressed, the energy of attitudes, vibes, and tones clearly communicate our beliefs and expectations.

My own experience attests to these findings. From my third year of teaching on, my high-risk classes not only met the standards, but also achieved an average advancement of 2.5 to 3 years, despite the students diagnoses, labels, and some having lost one year's growth with previous teachers, as described in AcademicSuccess101.com.

> Before you can change anybody else,
> you must first change yourself!

If we believe Johnny is a loser, or that Suzy will flake out, or Matt won't concentrate and do the work, it will most likely turn out precisely as predicted.

Why? Because our thoughts and feelings—our vibes—carry tremendous energetic influence. Our beliefs invite those around us to act in accordance with the expected outcome.

The students in these experiments, as well as the adults in your life, are strongly affected by the energy of your expectations. (And trust me on this: some of your colleagues and adult family

members may have many of the same issues and labels that cate-
gorize youth as "at-risk!")

So when you are having difficulty communicating with a child, take time to get truly honest with yourself about your underlying attitudes, biases, and labels.

Is it a "given" that Amy is just as much of a slow learner as her older sibling? Is Jared a born troublemaker? Stop and recognize that those attitudes are being projected to the world, like a neon sign on your forehead.

Owning what you discover deep inside of yourself is the most transformative thing you can do for yourself and those you are trying to get through to.

Less Effort, Better Results

Stop trying so hard to get kids to "get it." Take a breath! *Lean in* and keep every conversation in the AFZ: Attitude Free Zone.

So be the first. Be the Adult. Pull that attitude of yours back in and rewrite the script. You will begin to see incredible and inspiring results from the children you are working with.

I understand that this may be overwhelming for you on the one hand. On the other hand, it may be the relief you've been waiting for because it really explains why you are never without power.

It's a relief to know that it's not your lack of skills, but rather it's something as simple as your attitude that is keeping you from being an effective teacher, parent, mentor, or helping professional.

Either way, it is essential to lean in to what you really think, without guilt. Keep in mind that, up until now, you have been doing the best you could in all of this, simply not knowing the powerful implications of the attitudes you have held in the past.

Now, with this understanding, not only can you take your power back energetically, but you can also deliberately and intentionally begin to transform energy. You'll thereby solicit different energetic responses from the children you're having difficulties with. As a bonus, you'll discover that you'll now have a beneficial effect on the circumstances and situations that are unsettling.

You see, we don't get an exact computer printout of what others are thinking or feeling, and it's best that we don't. I really don't want to know all of the particulars about what you are or aren't thinking, feeling, or holding in your mind about me.

I can see it, feel it, and hear it in your attitudes, vibes, and tones. That's generally more than enough incoming information for me to decide upon a response that I can return vibrationally that will, in fact, affect the energy between us. The same process applies to our relationship with students.

Suppose you are exhausted with "certain" kids in your classroom or family. In that case, it is most likely your judgment, bias, and labeling getting in your way—de-energizing you and inadvertently pushing them away. It's not only making your life harder; it's limiting the very child you wish to help.

What I did with Brandon in my B-Mod exercise only took 30 seconds, once I let down my defenses and allowed myself to reach in and find an infinitesimal bias that was getting in the way of all my efforts.

So, give yourself permission to know what you need to know. It takes only a moment of your time. There are no attitude police to tell you that you're a bad person for whatever bias you may be harboring.

See if you can't get to the heart of whatever it is you dislike so intensely about this child. I only felt different when I was working with him. That's all. He felt it, and he eventually leaned into my vibe and began to trust me more. It had a direct impact on his ability to think and to learn.

Let's take a moment to examine how my 3 Energy Hacks were in play, long before I realized it.

High Vibe It: Brandon's behavior, or the lack thereof, was a flashing sign: YOUR ENERGY IS! He was mirroring my bias because Vibes Don't Lie.

What, If, When It: When I settled into B-Mod-ing myself about this, I was essentially doing my *What, If, When It* on myself. I got real with myself about what I really thought.

ReLabel It: In this situation the relabeling happened instantaneously. Recognizing that my bias was creating an energetic chasm between us and that it was rooted in my perceptions rather than any factual basis, I understood that my energetic message contradicted my "rah-rah come on you can do it" lecture.

In examining Brandon's behavior through the lens of my 3 Energy Hacks, it's clear that our energies were deeply interconnected.

Having the courage to simply "own" my biases—within myself—helped me align my energetic message with my intentions. By fostering self-awareness and authenticity, we can bridge gaps in communication and promote meaningful change in our interactions.

CHAPTER 20

FROM INVISIBLE TO INVINCIBLE

Rising Above Being Overlooked and Undervalued

As we transition from Brandon's journey to Roger's transformation, we continue to explore how my 3 Energy Hacks play a pivotal role in transforming behavior and fostering resilience.

Roger, a seventh grader grappling with feelings of invisibility and unwantedness, embodies the challenges many face when seeking support. In this chapter, we'll uncover how Annabelle's experiences with Roger reflect the foundational principles established in our previous discussions.

By applying the practices of *High Vibe It, What, If, When It,* and *ReLabel It,* Annabelle shares how she navigates the complexities of Roger's core beliefs. In applying what she was learning about energetics, she ultimately helps him emerge from the shadows of self-doubt and into a place of empowerment and synergistic connection.

Let's delve into her inspiring case study and witness the transformative power of these energetic strategies in action.

Through Annabelle's dedication, Roger's evolution from feeling invisible to embracing his potential inspires others to prioritize emotional well-being and engage constructively with their surroundings, highlighting the profound impact of energetic support.

In Annabelle's Own Words: The Transformation of Roger

Annabelle McGuire Case Study for *Energetics of Behavior*
(formerly *Breaking Cycles of Failure*),
Portland State University CEU Course
—Multnomah County ESD—
Instructor Mary Robinson Reynolds

"Attempting to make a difference with some individuals can be an extremely difficult, unrewarding, and demanding task in the early stages. The most difficult aspect for me has been the idea that I need to generate affirmative thoughts or attitudes about the person involved before I can make an impact. I need to believe in an individual and have an optimistic vision for them before I can expect a beneficial outcome. This is quite a task when the individual doesn't shower you with positive feedback because he doesn't believe in himself. I have learned, however, that *Makin' Magic* works, with persistence.

"I have been doing a case study the past nine weeks of this training, using one of my twelve-year-old 7th grade social studies/language arts students. His name is Roger. I picked Roger because he is a silent one who will fall through the cracks of school bureaucracy if he doesn't get help quickly. He is not violent, vulgar, or angry. He is not a typical, loud and boisterous, attention-demanding twelve-year-old. His pleas for help are quiet and subtle. He breathes unwantedness and incompetence. I have actually been working with Roger since last fall when I began to notice this child who didn't care much about school, let alone himself. I have tried desperately to seek out ways to inspire him. His lack of success and unhappy nature have been nagging at me ever since I met him.

"Earlier in the year, I approached Roger with doubt and contrived encouragement. I was a good example of frustration. This was exactly what Roger was used to. Frustrated adults nagging at him to do things he knew would never meet their expectations. I directly reinforced his negative core belief of incompetence and unintentionally made him feel unwanted.

"Even though I was putting a significant amount of emotional energy into this child, it wasn't doing any good. I verbally nagged Roger, wrote passes requiring him to come in at lunch, called his nagging mother, conveyed disappointment to him when he didn't follow through, had him design a behavior contract which he, his mother, and I signed. Amid all this negative energy, I wasn't able to see the core beliefs that Roger was harboring. It's no wonder we didn't get along.

"It is now plain as day for me to see the negativism that surrounds Roger's spirit. With this knowledge, I have been rejuvenated and have found a new passage to Roger's spirit. I am optimistic.

"Roger's most obvious negative core beliefs about himself are that he is unwanted and incompetent. When I talk with Roger and work with him now, I intentionally focus on the opposites of those beliefs and convey that message to him.

"I tell him that he is talented. I tell him that I enjoy having him come to my room to work. I tell him that I sincerely care about him and want him to be happy. I tell him that he is competent and loved. I show him these feelings by sitting with him at the same table in the mornings. I give him extra pats on the back for completing the assignment with little assistance.

"And the assistance that I was giving him was no more than what any other child might need. I believed that he could complete assignments and would complete them to the best of his ability. This attitude and belief created and fueled my new attitude and response to Roger. It was a bit like a miracle to see the changes in Roger.

"However, it has taken about eight weeks for there to be noticeable change in Roger, as Mary indicated it would.

"It is now quite easy for me to visualize myself in a positive, new response. I believe in Roger, so the new, more optimistic response comes easily.

"Virtually everything I say to him is somehow related to *What, If, When It,* 'I really care about you,' and 'this is really good stuff.' He honestly seems to want this because he keeps coming back for more. His level of commitment is now active. When we first met, he didn't care. There was no reason for commitment. Occasionally he dips into passivity but overall, he seems to enjoy being active and now he has a reason to be active.

"Roger is now keeping up with all assignments in my class and spends extra time in my room on his own. He is an inspiration to others. My attitude about Roger has changed significantly since last fall. I have learned that he is very capable, and I have learned to really care about him. I hope that I have provided him with the tools and confidence to believe in himself. These he will need to maintain his active level of commitment." *Names have been changed.

Let's Unpack This

As we conclude our exploration of Annabelle's inspiring case study with Roger, let's take a moment to reflect on how she effectively utilized my 3 Energy Hacks: *High Vibe It, What, If, When It,* and *ReLabel It*. These strategies were crucial in bringing about his remarkable transformation.

High Vibe It: First, let's discuss how Annabelle created a welcoming atmosphere. From the outset, she recognized that her initial energy was tinged with frustration, doubt, and contrived encouragement. However, she consciously shifted her mindset, embracing a more nurturing and optimistic attitude, vibe, and tone. She celebrated even the smallest victories for Roger, consistently reinforcing his strengths. Take note here: this focus on her own energy and affirmative language is key. By encouraging Roger and making a deliberate attempt to genuinely believe in his potential, she crafted an energetic environment that fostered his self-worth and motivated him to engage in learning.

What, If, When It: Now, let's delve into the *What, If, When Method*. Annabelle shared with me that she used this method to help Roger regulate his feelings and behaviors. When faced with a perplexing situation, she first asked, "What's going on for you that you did that thing that you did?" This direct question aimed to get to the heart of the matter. If Roger struggled to articulate his thoughts, she would then gently prompt him with, "If you did know, what might it be?" This open-ended inquiry encouraged him to dig deeper and explore his feelings. And if he still found himself at a loss, Annabelle assured him, "When you do know, let's talk." This approach not only validated his experiences but also gave him the space to reflect without pressure.

By using this method, Annabelle avoided the urge to jump in early to fix things for Roger—an approach that vibrationally transmits "I don't believe in you to find your own answers." Instead, she empowered him to take ownership of his emotions and actions, fostering self-awareness and encouraging personal growth.

ReLabel It: Finally, we must highlight how Annabelle effectively applied the relabeling technique. She understood that Roger's self-identification as "unwanted" and "incompetent" was holding him back. Through their collaboration, she guided him to relabel these core beliefs. By helping him see himself as "a thoughtful observer with unique insights," she facilitated a transformative process that changed his self-perception. Relabeling is a powerful strategy; it allows individuals to break free from limiting narratives and embrace a new identity filled with possibility.

As we wrap this up, let's appreciate how Annabelle's deliberate use of these 3 Energy Hacks not only transformed Roger's life but also exemplifies how effective teaching can make a profound difference.

By creating a *High Vibe It* environment, exploring hopeful possibilities and facilitating relabeling, she has shown us that with the right tools and mindset we can ignite the latent potential in every student.

Remember, these strategies are not just theoretical concepts; they are practical tools we can all employ in our own interactions to uplift and empower those around us.

Something To Think About

As we conclude Part II of this journey into *Change Your Vibe*, it's essential to reflect on the profound impact our attitudes and expectations have on the lives of the children we influence.

Through the lens of my experience with Brandon and Annabelle's experience with Roger, we have seen how our deeply embedded beliefs can unknowingly create barriers to our students' success.

By recognizing and shifting these attitudes, we can foster an environment where every child feels valued and empowered to thrive. Remember, the energy we project shapes not only our interactions but also the outcomes we witness.

Drawing from my forty years of experience in finding simpler, more effective ways to support today's children, the strategies I'm sharing may seem unorthodox. While everyone could benefit from these methods, many remain unaware of how simple they are to implement.

Please don't underestimate the life-changing power of my 3 Energy Hacks; they remain my go-to tools for turning around unproductive situations in 30 seconds or less, more often than not.

As we move forward, let us embrace this knowledge and become intentional in our efforts to uplift and inspire, paving the way for meaningful connections and transformations in the chapters ahead.

Now that we've explored the significance of understanding our children's reflections, let's move on to the next exciting section of this book: *See Kids Thrive.*

PART III:

SEE YOUR KIDS THRIVE

Operative word is SEE.

Quick question: How does a person SEE something in a way that is different from what it currently is?

Quick answer: You Relabel it to SEE the highest and best possible outcome or experience.

BEGIN WITH THE END IN MIND: SEE IT FIRST

CHAPTER 21

IS WHAT YOU SEE WHAT YOU GET?

> "When a flower doesn't bloom,
> you fix the environment in which it grows.
> Not the flower."
>
> -Alexander Den Heijer

The problem is that our children are not broken. We just *see* them and treat them as if they are. What we believe shapes what we see, as our beliefs are seeds that we plant, water, and nourish vibrationally in our minds. An adult's belief, attitude, vibe, and tone are everything. It's the cornerstone of everything that comes after.

What's wrong, more often than not, is that the energetic environment we immerse children in, particularly those with problematic behaviors or learning styles, is often untenable for them.

Children—by the very fact that they are children—are unskilled at problem-solving, communicating, and meeting expectations at an adult level. How do you fix what's not broken?

Let's keep going so we can learn how to see better the cues each individual's neurological wiring is signaling with new eyes of understanding.

Diagnoses and labels justify additional academic assistance and emotional support for children with problematic behaviors, unskillful communication, and learning style differences.

However, without relabeling the meanings assigned to them, it remains a double-edge sword which will become a self-fulling prophecy, as we've learned from Brandon's story in Chapter 18.

Now, consider the labels we assign to behaviors. It's only natural to try to decode actions we don't understand. Yet, these labels are often seductive traps. After all, labeling behaviors affects our understanding of not just the behavior itself but the essence of the child exhibiting it.

For example, the well known terms "terrible twos," "troublesome threes" are blanket classifications that can freeze a child in a framework of negativity from an early age. Similarly, the "impossible or hormonal teens" labels slot adolescents into a box, creating assumptions and fostering relationships mired in misunderstanding.

Here's some more we use without thinking of their energetically infusing implications: brat, challenging, problem, willful, difficult, hard, defiant, strong-willed, contrary, bad, stupid, never listens, mouthy, hostile, needy, too sensitive, angry, lazy, manipulator, liar, stubborn, complex, and spirited (a *socially sensitive* way to refer to a child who may be perceived as difficult, challenging, or demanding, particularly in the context of behavior that might include hyperactivity, impulsivity, or being hard to manage).

Now, I realize that I may have upset the apple cart by including "challenging" in this list. This term represents the newest, latest, greatest, *socially sensitive* language used to describe children today who do not fit into the proverbial box of compliant learners prepared to engage with traditional neurotypical, right-brained methods.

How you SEE something is how you've LABELED it!

My relabels for "terrible twos," "troublesome threes," and "impossible or hormonal teens" are "sweet, sweet twos," "terrific threes," and "adventuresome, self-advocating teens."

Here's the thing. When my son was two, and he'd start having a meltdown, I would say, "Where's my sweet, sweet boy?" I'd look all around the room, and say, "I don't see him. Where did he go?" "Where's my sweet, sweet boy?" And he'd run up to me and say, "Here I am mommy, here I am!"

But that's not the end of this story: over the years, the number one compliment I would receive when people would find out he was my son is, "Your son is the sweetest young man I've ever met."

To this day, this is what people say about him and his sons.

So, you may have a child that is anything but sweet right now in your home or classroom, but the dividends are in the making if you will just stop using labels that are getting you everything you do not want.

The Language We Use:
Rethinking Labels and Their Effects on Young Minds

If someone labeled you as "challenging," "stubborn," "strong-willed," or "spirited" how would you feel about yourself? But it's not just that. How big is the energetic chasm between you and them every time you have to live or work with them from now on?

What's your internal dialogue like now?

And let's not forget our #1 label: ADHD—Attention Deficit Hyperactive Disorder. Everywhere you turn, somebody's naming and claiming it to be their reason for how they are showing up for their lives and responsibilities, or not!

Anyone using screens these days can be said to have ADHD. Put down your phone for 30 days, then have another SPECT brain scan, and let's see if you aren't better. If you are not better, then do the work to retrain—rewire—your brain. There are books on how to do it. I've done it. Stop being a victim of your own making and stop teaching students and children in your home, helplessness. What we are modeling every moment of every day is something to think about!

I really appreciate the work of Eric Jensen in his book *Teaching with Poverty in Mind: What Being Poor Does to Kids' Brains and What Schools Can Do About It.* During one of the webinars I attended, he shared that he underwent several SPECT brain scans. In one of the scans, he viewed highly agitating and stressful visual stimuli, and the results indicated that his brain appeared disordered, as if he could have been diagnosed with multiple disorders.

In contrast, when he watched soothing footage, his brain scan looked completely different—showing that his brain was functioning smoothly and effectively. Same brain, different results! This really drove home for me how profoundly our experiences and environments can shape our brain activity and functioning.

My point is this: let's not miss the forest for the trees here. I'm not denying that brain disorders exist, but based on the explosive study in Chapter 17 it suggests that we are labeling—diagnosing—today's children far too young. These labels can be, and most times are, life-limiting. We often overlook the messages children are receiving from the adults in their lives and the energetic pressure they deal with day in and day out.

Instead of rushing to label and diagnose, I think we need to ask ourselves 1) what are the energetics of their environment, and 2) what skills do these children simply need to be taught and helped to develop. Let's focus on that first.

It's been said:

Everything that follows "I AM" energetically chases you!

I AM ADHD disordered. I AM stupid. I AM bad. I AM broken. I AM helpless. I AM hopeless. I AM not good enough, pretty enough, thin enough.

Let's put I AM in front of each of these: challenging, a problem, willful, difficult, hard, spirited, complex, defiant, strong-willed, contrary, bad, stupid, a non-listener, mouthy, hostile, needy, too-sensitive, angry, lazy, a manipulator, stubborn, liar, a brat.

On a scale of 1-10, with 10 being the highest, where's your energy right now?

Versus:

I AM safe. I AM good. I AM loved. I AM enough. I AM well able. I AM focused. I AM wanted. I AM welcome. I AM gifted and talented in my own right. I AM smart. I AM creative. I AM responsible. I AM a leader. I AM healthy, happy, and fulfilled.

On a scale of 1-10, where's your energy now?

Here's my point:

As we've seen in the IKEA Experiment #2, we understand the actual effects of vibrational frequencies associated with hurtful words—labels—on living things.

In the context of relabeling today's children, this experiment serves as a powerful illustration of how the vibrational frequencies of our thoughts and the language we use to define and describe children directly impact their development and self-perception.

Just as the Dracaena plants responded to words—energy—of praise and criticism, children also absorb the labels placed upon them by adults, peers, and even societal norms.

Relabeling involves shifting the narrative surrounding children's behaviors, capabilities, and emotional responses. Instead of viewing anxious or explosive behaviors as inherent flaws or signs of weakness, we can redefine them as signals of energetic resistance—YOUR ENERGY IS—indications that require understanding, support, and action.

The words we use in this relabeling process hold immense vibrational power. By consciously highlighting strengths, encouraging growth, and recognizing efforts, we create an energetic environment that parallels the thriving plant in the experiment —one where children feel seen, valued, and empowered to flourish.

In many ways, today's children are often categorized and labeled based on how they are innately neurologically wired to engage in

      CHANGE YOUR VIBE, SEE YOUR KIDS THRIVE

their schoolwork and learn, which can be influenced by their susceptibility to energy and may result in behavioral issues, such as impulsivity or difficulty concentrating.

The new all-encompassing labels for learning differences are neurodivergent and neurotypical. I understand that parents are trying to encourage educators, relatives, and judgmental onlookers to stop pigeonholing their children simply because they are neuro-logically wired differently from other kids in any given classroom or public setting.

This newly acceptable *socially sensitive* labeling practice can trap them in a cycle of negativity, similar to the bullied plant, where the weight of disparaging words and life-limiting labels overshadows their potential.

To break this cycle, we must actively engage in relabeling, replacing critical or dismissive language with affirmations and constructive guidance.

Instead of labeling a child difficult, spirited, defiant, or strong-willed, we can change our language to reflect that they are creative, self-advocating, a future leader, or passionate, recognizing that these traits can be channeled positively.

This revision aligns with the findings of the IKEA experiment, which show that our words can foster growth or stifle it.

Something To Think About

Our ability to SEE our children THRIVE begins with the meaning we give behaviors and with reversing the labels we have been in-advertently assigning. Most people think their labels for each other are funny or that they are saying them lovingly with endearment.

I understand that. I hope after today you will think more about this. For example, while it seems cute to call a little girl "Miss Sassy Pants"—think ahead to her teenage years. Is this the seed you want to plant, nurture, and grow?

Relabeling extends beyond individual interactions; it demands a systemic shift in how society views childhood opportunities for growth and skill development. By cultivating a culture that prioritizes compassion and understanding, we provide children not only a fertile ground for growth but also a new identity. This encourages them to see themselves through a lens of empowerment, much like the complimented plant that flourished under nurturing words.

Ultimately, just as the energy directed towards the plants had tangible consequences, so too does the language and labeling we apply to children. By embracing a philosophy of relabeling, we can shift the current narrative surrounding today's children from one of anxiety and explosiveness to one of potential and resilience, ensuring they thrive rather than wither in the face of life's opportunities.

Whether we mean to be or not, we are all unequivocally projecting our thoughts upon children and each other all day every day.

> Eruptions are most likely to occur
> when what we think
> is what we expect,
> and often is what leads
> to what we get!

Or more broadly stated: Our thoughts and expectations play a significant role in shaping our experiences, often leading us to perceive outcomes in alignment with what we believe is possible.

CHAPTER 22

HEALING TODAY'S CHILDREN ... AND OURSELVES!

Are You Sacrificing Your Happiness
for Family Loyalty?

As we continue our exploration in Part III, *See Your Kids Thrive*, I can't help but think about the fascinating parallels between the 1970 Blakemore and Cooper Kitten Experiment and our own lives.

Our beliefs frame our understanding of the world,
but what if the very beliefs we hold
obscure the possibilities waiting to be discovered?

So, what do a bunch of kittens raised in two different worlds have to do with the deeply ingrained loyalties we hold toward our teachers, parents, peers, and our community-at-large?

The answer may surprise you.

Experiment #12 The Renowned Kitten Experiment

In Colin Blakemore and Grahame Cooper's Harvard University experiment, kittens were raised from birth in two separate physical environments. One group saw nothing but horizontal stripes, while the other saw vertical stripes.

Something remarkable happened. The cats raised with horizontal stripes could only see a horizontal world. They would walk into table legs as if they couldn't see them. On the other hand, the cats raised with vertical stripes could only see a vertical world, where they would walk off the edge of a step and fall, again as if they couldn't see the change in floor level

Why is this experiment so important?

It demonstrates the profound impact of our sensory experiences on our perception of the world. The cats' first sensory experience shapes their nervous system, making it difficult for them to perceive anything that doesn't align with their initial view.

In other words, what you see and believe to be true is largely a result of your past experiences.

Contrary to the saying, "seeing is believing," the evidence is just the opposite. Without a pre-existing belief or concept, your nervous system won't even allow new information to enter your mind.

There must be a neurological pathway for your brain to process and acknowledge it.

The mistake we often make as a society is that we double down on the answers we seek being an "either-or" (horizontal world vs vertical world), instead of creating a matrix of the best of both

 CHANGE YOUR VIBE, SEE YOUR KIDS THRIVE

worlds, i.e. parenting and teaching styles, all the way to politics, and religion. You get the idea, right?

However, you have the power to create new neurological pathways consciously through desire, feeling, and deliberate decision-making.

If you want to turn around your mindset, you must recognize the influence of your prior experiences. They have shaped how you see the world and yourself. But don't despair, because you possess the ability to break free from these limitations.

By consciously deciding to open your mind to new possibilities, you can forge new neurological pathways, allowing for a more expansive and empowering perspective, understanding, and compassion.

Reflecting on this experiment illuminates how our personal journeys have also been shaped by the environments we grew up in. Each one of us has been conditioned by the messages we've absorbed from our parents, teachers, peers, and society-at-large.

The ways we perceive our world—be it horizontally or vertically—stem from our upbringing.

Those formative experiences chart a course for how we see ourselves and interact with others, often without us even realizing it.

Now let's dig into the critical theme of loyalty.

How a Timely Seminar Transformed My Understanding of Love

As a high school counselor in 1985, I attended a talk on co-dependency given by Pia Melody, author of *Breaking Free: A Recovery Workbook for Facing Codependence*.

At that point in my life, I believed I had resolved my childhood wounds, but her message had a profound impact on me.

When Pia broke down the complex dynamics of love and loyalty —particularly how we sometimes conflate abuse with love—it became clear to me how deep-seated loyalty can keep us tethered to the pain inflicted by those we love.

Like the kittens that can't adjust to a different visual landscape as grown cats, many of us remain trapped in a cycle of acceptance regarding the hurt caused by those we are loyal to.

I'll never forget a conversation at my high school reunion, where a classmate recounted how her parents abused her by throwing her head into the wall when she was being "bad."

She brushed it off as though it was normal, insisting, "Oh, I deserved it." In that moment, I realized how often we rational-ize harmful behaviors in the name of loyalty.

What struck me that day was the realization that this is not love; it is a distortion—a trap that keeps us stuck in the generational legacy of inflicting pain to teach a lesson. All "in the name of love?" I think not.

We all know love is patient. Love is kind. It doesn't dishonor others. It is not easily angered. It keeps no record of wrongs.

Recognizing this pattern changed my life forever, but it required a *willingness* to confront hard truths and break free from the limitations of my previous beliefs.

That was the day I stopped giving my parents a free pass into my psyche. And yes, over time, I learned how to confront abusive default adulting non-confrontationally

I became an adult who was able to call out hurtful, harmful behavior not just for me, but for the kids I was advocating for.

So what about our relationships with our parents?

Are we expected to sever those bonds for self-protection and emotional well-being?

Not necessarily.

In fact, gaining insight into their "old-school" authoritarian mindset and learning to disagree with it didn't damage my connection with them; instead, it liberated me from the misconception that I deserved their harmful treatment.

Not only that, but because I learned how to confront them non-confrontationally, they never used their abusive tactics on me or my son again. My energy was firm and fair. My energetic message to them was, "Don't even!"

Let your energy do the talking!

This newfound understanding empowered me to confront not only my parents but also two mean-spirited, abusive aunts who felt entitled to unleash their unfiltered and intentionally hurtful criticism on anyone they deemed deserved it.

The Work of Healing Ourselves

Whether you are a classroom teacher, parent, or principal, our children mirror our attitudes, vibes, and tones, and they are essentially some version of our little mini-Mes.

By now, you may recognize that through the children in our lives, we have the opportunity to confront and heal past childhood wounds, rather than subjecting ourselves to further anguish.

It's been said that "love brings up that which most needs to be healed." If this is new information for you, opportunity after opportunity will appear for you to stand up for children in your life, as a way of healing yourself from the times you felt that you could not stand up for yourself.

It's not a matter of "if" it's a matter of "when."

Becoming Our Parents

It's the moment you realize you're reacting to a situation like your parent did, launching into the familiar patterns that they used on you. At that point, you can choose to wake up and break the cycle or stay asleep, passing on the emotional burdens to the next generation.

It's that moment when your parents' frustration will come up from your gut, up through your throat and out of your mouth if you don't stop yourself.

It's that moment when you become like a broken record repeating everything that was said to you, launching it at vulnerable young minds.

This is your defining moment.

Will you brush it off, saying "Well they did it to me, and I turned out OK?" Or will you do the work to learn better—more humane—ways to be the adult who empowers, encourages, and teaches skills instead of using threats and punitive measures to teach a lesson?

There are several insurance company commercials running right now about how not to become your parents. They've done a great job demonstrating helicopter parenting.

Because I was my parents' designated problem child, I recognized this in my students long before becoming a parent. I could empathetically feel my students' pain and suffering.

I'll never forget that day in my first year of teaching when that pivotal moment came. I heard myself become my mother. It was a defining moment, and I decided to not do to children what had been done to me. I was going to commit to learning better ways.

Each step of the way, I found myself heal just a little bit more as I reached back into my own childhood to treat them the way I wish I would have been treated.

Then came my own children, and it was even more intense than I had ever imagined. The healing I needed to do for myself came through my very own mini-Me son and amazing bonus daughters. There were times when they mirrored back to me wounded parts of my psyche and soul, and at those moments I'd know what to do.

Our three children are gifted, talented, and deeply humane adults, living their very best, productive lives. Not only did we blend two families, but we also worked harmoniously with our former spouses.

For those who doubt a kinder form of raising children, as in "Firm, Fair, Fearless, Flexible, Focused, Forthright, and—most impor- tantly—FUNctional" parenting, our children exemplify its success. One advanced a grade, another performed as "Dorothy," and one graduated as valedictorian, showcasing their unique talents.

All three thrived in high school and successfully put themselves through college, with two graduating magna cum laude and one earning summa cum laude honors. The point being, they achieved all this without fear, threats, pressure, or force, but rather encouragement and support over punitive measures. Our experience shows that compassionate guidance fosters self-motivation and leads to remarkable academic accomplishments and fulfilling lives. I could easily write a book about the joy they are.

Loyalty Must Be Earned

I invite you to reflect on who you're being loyal to and why.

Are these relationships enriching your life, or are they undeserved burdens?

It takes energetic clarity and resolve to stand up to the adults in our world who have been hurtful and harmful. These individuals often feel unapologetically entitled to be as abusive, disapproving, and as punitive as they want, carrying their generational trauma forward into this next generation.

But more importantly, it takes skill to effectively call them out and courage to put a stop to the hurtful ways once and for all.

It's time to confront this loyalty that we bear toward our former caregivers, not through "all up in your business" attitudinal confrontation, but rather by employing my non-confrontational approach.

Go see my *What, If, When Method* and *7 Best One Liners* Micro-Dose resources, or better yet my *Victim No More* Macro-Dose Online Course. All three are quick and easy programs that encourage non-confrontational dialogue and intercession on hurtful behaviors. You can them find at: MaryReynolds.com/Programs

CHAPTER 23

INTELLIGENT DISOBEDIENCE

Intelligent Disobedience is an intriguing training technique wherein service animals are permitted, and even encouraged, to disregard their handler's commands to prioritize safety. The allowance of their instinctive behavior is a vital part of their training, enabling them to effectively assist their owners.

These remarkable animals learn to assess their environment, weigh the potential outcomes of obeying commands, and choose a safer course of action if need be. For example, a service dog may refuse to proceed when a blind owner approaches a busy street, thereby prioritizing their handler's well-being over compliance.

In our roles as educators and parents, we similarly bear the responsibility of guiding our children within established rules and processes.

However, there are critical moments when diverging from the status quo is essential for fostering problem-solving, collaboration, synergy, community, and unity.

In today's increasingly complex world, an essential skill to teach our children is the ability to confidently and respectfully disobey authority when necessary.

Intelligent Disobedience can also be applied to children in the context of their behavior and decision-making.

When children question rules or authority, it may indicate that they are thinking critically about their environment or the directives given to them. This critical thinking is an essential skill that fosters independence and problem-solving abilities.

Instead of viewing a child's questioning or refusal to follow orders as simple disobedience, parents and educators can interpret it as a sign of developing discernment and reasoning skills.

Moreover, children may sometimes refuse to comply with directives when they sense that a request may not be in their best interest, even if they're not fully aware of the reasons.

For example, a child might refuse to go somewhere they feel uncomfortable or unsafe, which can be viewed as a form of Intelligent Disobedience. In this light, understanding their perspective is essential for guiding them in making thoughtful decisions and ensuring their safety by learning to trust their intuition.

Allowing children the space to express their opinions and challenge instructions respectfully can empower them. Encouraging Intelligent Disobedience fosters confidence in their judgment and promotes open communication, making them feel heard and valued.

However, it is equally vital to teach children about boundaries, authority, and the appropriate contexts in which questioning

     CHANGE YOUR VIBE, SEE YOUR KIDS THRIVE

authority is acceptable. This balance helps them learn discernment and judgment in their responses.

Additionally, children who demonstrate Intelligent Disobedience may be exhibiting emotional intelligence, as they can recognize their own and others' feelings. This understanding can lead them to make decisions that prioritize their own well-being or that of those around them.

Adults can demonstrate Intelligent Disobedience by respectfully questioning rules or discussing ethical concerns, helping children learn when and how to challenge norms skillfully.

Overall, recognizing that a child's disobedience might stem from a place of thoughtful perspective rather than mere defiance allows caregivers to engage in more constructive conversations. This approach not only helps in guiding children's behavior but also nurtures their cognitive and emotional development.

In essence, it transforms what others may perceive as defiance into a powerful tool for empowerment and social evolution. Yet this notion presents a challenge for many authority figures.

Parents and teachers who struggle with it often operate under a "Because I said so!" mentality—an approach steeped in authoritarianism. Ironically, what they often perceive as disrespect may actually stem from their own disrespectful use of force rather than a true respect for the children in their charge.

Former Problem Child

It all began for me as my parents' problem child—or, as I like to say, FPC: Former Problem Child.

Reflecting on my own caustic childhood, I made a point to teach and model for children precisely how they could respectfully self-advocate successfully with me.

This intention developed during my first year as an educator, as I strived to advance from an authoritarian to an authoritative approach.

Instead of crushing their attempts at self-advocacy with hurtful sarcasm, shame, and humiliation, I taught them how to be heard and taken seriously by the adults in their lives.

My experience gives me a unique lens—an instinctual insight—into what's truly going on inside the minds and hearts of so many children today who are blowing past social norms and creating chaos in schools and homes.

With alarming rises in violence, addiction, and suicide rates, it is evident that many kids are desperately seeking ways to assert their voices when they sense something is off, hurtful, harmful, or unnecessary coming from adults and peers in their lives.

At the heart of this issue lies the cornerstone of energetics—the attitudes, vibes, and tones that adults wield to shame, dismiss, crush, and control children. All too often, this approach backfires, pushing kids even further away.

This tumultuous backdrop can empower adults to engage young minds meaningfully, cultivating an environment where self-advocacy is not only encouraged but celebrated.

You may wonder what I did to earn that "problem child" label.

Knowing what I know now, I would have to say the problem was that I was simply an outside-the-box thinker, creative, and neurologically wired to lead. I advocated for myself, discerningly challenging the authority of adults around me. My Intelligent Disobedience was alive and well.

Watch Out for Mary

After I became a teacher, my mother shared that at the beginning of each school year, she would go to school to introduce herself to my new teacher. She would make it clear that she would only believe about half of the stories I brought home if the teacher would believe about half of the stories I told at school!

My mother didn't do this for me; she did it out of her own embarrassment about what I might or might not do. When introducing me to people, she referred to me with a hint of trepidation, saying, "This is Mary, our 'adopted' daughter."

This introduction was not one of pride as one might expect, but rather presented as a warning—an unspoken caution that effectively said, "She is not of our blood, and we're not responsible for whatever she does next."

That stigma stayed with me. Each school year began with me replaying the thoughts of "What have I done wrong?" I could never figure out why my teachers appeared not to like me from day one.

This energetic chasm in the middle of every conversation left me anxious and bewildered. It fueled endless rumination as I tried to understand what was so fundamentally wrong with me and often made focusing in class nearly impossible.

By age 16, I turned to "closet smoking" to find some calm—a habit I cloaked in shame. The energetic rejection I felt from educators stung deeply, culminating in frequent headaches—not due to any physical ailment, but from the mental scolding I poured upon myself for every inadvertent misstep.

What had I done to warrant such concern and disappointment from my parents?

Ultimately, I was just a normal kid with insights and wisdom beyond my years.

I confronted the shaming and humiliating tactics directed at me, bravely voicing my disagreements—each time earning a swift slap across my face for "talking back." In truth, that was the very essence of my Intelligent Disobedience in action.

The "Not As Smart As Your Sister" Effect

Despite the hurdles I faced, I pursued education, even though I struggled academically after third grade. So, what happened in third grade? I received my very first B, and on the way home, my mother attempted to console me by saying, "It's okay; we don't expect you to be as smart as your sister."

Until that point, I had no idea I wasn't as smart!

That comment took root in my thinking, and learning became much harder for me, significantly altering the trajectory of my life.

Thankfully, my intelligence was fully restored fifteen years later while working toward my master's degree (see my story at MaryReynolds.com/Sister).

I'm not the first person to enter education to heal from a painful childhood, nor will I be the last. I'll never forget when that pivotal moment arrived in my first year of teaching. I'd signed on to teach a class of twenty-eight students combining grades 3, 4, 5, and 6.

One day, while observing kids simply being kids, it struck me: I had never been the problem; I was a perfectly normal child with age-related behaviors who simply needed affirmation and understanding.

If we want to improve our lives and relationships with children to improve, we must be willing to interrupt our patterns, atone for our tones, and sincerely apologize for any harm we may unintentionally cause.

Our Children Are Watching

It requires us to open ourselves to new learning, reset our DARP—Default Adulting Response Patterns—and break the generational legacy of pain.

The answers we seek often lie within the dynamic interplay between what we think we know and what remains to be discovered.

We must stop JREDDing:

JUSTIFY, RATIONALIZE, EXPLAIN, DEFEND, and DEBATE.

Let this be your invitation to expand your view, adjust the lens with which you currently see things, just like we learned in the kitten experiment.

When we bring together the horizontal and vertical worlds —allowing space for growth, change, and healing—we can create a life filled with clarity, compassion, and joy.

So, let's step off that beaten path of misguided loyalty and embark on a journey toward authentic connections and an empowered life.

Today is your day to rise—don't let past experiences dictate your future. Choose love that uplifts and empowers. Choose to be free.

And above all else, ease into this.

> The energetic presence of
> certainty, authority, and confidence
> comes from practice, practice, practice.

The energy of certainty that you show up with in every situation does the work for you. How do you increase your level of certainty in your mind, in advance, so that your AFZ: Attitude Free Zone is being energetically clean, kind, firm, fair, and FUNctional?

Show up for your life and open your arms wide each day. Make it your mission to command the room with your grace, light, love, and energy.

Know that you have something valuable to offer.

Be resolved about who you are.

> Remember, energy first, tools second.

CHAPTER 24

FROM LEMONS TO LEMONADE

When life gives you lemons,
ask for sugar and water too!

In my own experience, I encountered years of judgment from teachers who were hurtful and harmful. When the important people in my life—teachers, parents, sibling, peers, and coaches—wielded sarcasm like a weapon, the energy of their condescension created a ripple effect among my peers.

The judgment didn't just affect at me; it influenced how others perceived and interacted with me as well.

This is not just my story; it is the story of far too many children we are losing through the cracks of our schools and communities.

We inadvertently perpetuate a system that dismisses their needs and misreads their behaviors as right or wrong, good or bad.

Instead of focusing on skill development, collaboration, and compassion, overlooking these opportunities, we often see these children as needing threats or harsh punishment to teach a lesson.

By failing to recognize the energetic dynamics at play, we overlook the profound impact our words, attitudes, and DARP—Default Adulting Response Patterns—have on their lives. Every sarcastic comment, every judgmental "look," and every moment of indifference and ghosting chips away at their self-worth and potential.

As we navigate this complex landscape, it's crucial to understand how our interactions shape the emotional climate of our classrooms and homes. If we genuinely seek to empower our youth, we must become more intentional in fostering relationships that affirm rather than diminish.

We must manage our own behavioral responses first, if we are to model respect and regard.

It is my hope that my "explosive" lemonade story will shine a light on the importance of understanding energetics and how we can transform our environments to uplift, rather than alienate, the children who need us to seek understanding the most.

Today's Children Blowing Past Social Norms

As we examine the rising tide of children exploding in classrooms and homes, it's clear that the energetics of both peers and adults play a pivotal role in these emotional outbursts.

Negative, judgmental attitudes and the heavy vibes transmitted through tone and body language create an inflammatory environment, often igniting explosive behavior in our youth.

Imagine a classroom where sarcasm and disdain linger in the air— each dismissive glance and harsh word compounds the pressure on energetically attuned—intuitive—kids, leading to implosions growing into explosions that disrupt learning and relationships.

When children feel this negative energy, they often lash out, seeking an outlet for the frustration and pain inflicted by their environments.

But here's the transformative insight: by consciously shifting our energy toward empathy, understanding, and encouragement, we can create a space that fosters connection and resilience. This isn't just wishful thinking; it's a necessity. When adults and peers project welcoming energy and support, even the most vulnerable children can thrive.

> I know what that moment of "no return" feels like
> to explode and completely blow past social norms
> and then feel humiliated and justified at the same time.

Mrs. A.

In my senior year, I was walking by the faculty break room and overheard Mrs. A. making soul crushing remarks about me to other teachers in the room. She was being openly disparaging, dismissive, and sarcastic trying to get a laugh from other adults in the room at my expense.

I'd endured this mean-spirited woman for six years as a home room teacher and in the required home economics classes. She was condescending, judgmental, sarcastic, skeptical, fault-finding, and as diminishing towards me as she could be. I had taken her hurtful energetic attitudinal hits and just walked on, never knowing what I'd ever done to attract such disdain and contempt from her.

But on this day, I'd had it.

Graduation was only a few months away. I walked across the hall to her Home Ec room and closed the door. Then I proceeded to take all of the dry goods off the shelves and sprinkle them all over the floor. I'd never done anything like this before in my life. I'd had it with this horrible person.

Radiating a big guilt vibe, just as I was leaving her classroom and closing the door, I ran into the school janitor.

I smiled and said "Hi" as I always did. Within an hour, my mother was called to the principal's office, as I was.

And so, the lecture began. "Didn't I know how wrong that was?" "What was I thinking!" Wah Wa Wa Wah Wa Wa.

But this time, I turned it around on them. I laid out my prosecutorial argument. I said that I deliberately and intentionally did what I did because it was the "principle" of the thing, and she should have to apologize to me for her hateful rhetoric in the teachers' lounge and years of undeserved sarcasm toward me!

They looked surprised at my well thought out argument. For a brief moment I thought maybe I should be a lawyer, I was laying out my case so well!

Shock! Dismay! Intelligent disobedience is what it was.

My mother and the principal tried hard to lecture me, but I could tell that neither one of them approved of what this teacher had done either. But being authoritarians, they stood united, determined to teach me a lesson I'd never forget by using public shaming and humiliation as my punishment. I was assigned many hours scraping gum off of the gymnasium bleachers after school.

To my knowledge Mrs. A. never received any reprimand, and she certainly never apologized to me.

Making Lemonade

Here's the kicker to this story. Because I am the creative, out-of-the-box thinker that I am, while scrapping gum that first afternoon, pushing down feeling humiliated in this way, I got a bright idea.

The school's Athletic Banquet was coming up, and I knew no one was stepping up to plan and organize it.

Having been the president of the student counsel and several other organizations in high school, I also knew there were very few resources for decorating, but in my mind's eye, I could see how I would decorate the very gymnasium I was scrapping gum in.

The school had rolls and rolls of colored paper in the stockroom. I could see the theme of Sesame Street with 6-foot A-Z alphabet letters in primary colors hanging from a wire the length of the gymnasium. We had just enough streamers for the other two sides of the gym, leaving the stage area open.

The next day, I went to the principal's office, and like Walt Disney, I created a full color drawing of my entire plan, and then asked if— for my penance—I could be put in charge of the Athletic Banquet?

I'd start by making the 6-foot-tall letters A-Z for the long wall. Oh, and I'd need to create the 6-foot letters on one of the cutting tables in Mrs. A.'s classroom after school.

To my surprise, he said yes, and made all the arrangements for me to have full run of the school building in the upcoming weeks leading up to the banquet.

Mrs. A. only appeared once in her classroom while I was designing and cutting the 26 letters. She came in while I was working, and I just smiled directly at her with the smile of a victor.

Something To Think About

Now my personal explosion story is small in comparison to what we are seeing happening in our schools and homes today.

Not every kid is going to rise up the way I did when someone has pushed them to the ground, put their foot on their shoulder holding them down, yelling at them to get up!

Yes, I am discerning, self-advocating, and an innovator.

This is a great story for me, but not every crushed, beat down student has the zeal to come up over the attitudinal vibes and tones of the adults in their world like I did.

So, students who have been exceedingly traumatized may become sour, dour, and depressed or hateful, angry, and ready to erupt.

My point here is that not every child can rise up without someone believing in them first.

I guess some would say that I was "strong-willed" or "stubborn," which are two labels I abhor and cringe every time I hear an adult labeling a child this way.

What you have is a "discerning leader in the making," a child who has the inherent chutzpah to be the change we all need to see.

That's why I do what I do. I want adults who love, live, and work with today's children to find better—more humane—ways to understand and respond to what children's behaviors are actually communicating.

CHAPTER 25

THE ECHOES OF JUDGMENT

How Adult Perceptions Shape a Child's Reality

In the complex arena of education, the often-unspoken energetics between adults and children can shape the very essence of a child's experience and development. In this chapter we delve into the profound impact that adult attitudes—manifested through labels and their unspoken cues, tones, and attitudes—can have on young minds.

When adults in positions of authority harbor fears or detrimental perceptions about children, they inadvertently create an atmosphere that is rife with misunderstanding and tension.

Through the poignant story of a young boy named Cory, we can explore how these subtle, yet powerful, vibrations may lead children to internalize harmful labels. We will see how these labels fueled Cory's feelings of inadequacy and anger, activating explosive and aggressive behaviors.

By recognizing and addressing the energetic undercurrents at play, we can initiate a transformative process that not only uplifts our children but also fosters a more compassionate and understanding educational environment for everyone.

Together, we will uncover the vital need for accountability among adults and the transformative potential of relabeling our perceptions to create a more nurturing space for growth and connection.

When A Child Is Labeled "Evil"

Cory was in first grade when I arrived at his school as counselor, and it wasn't long before teachers and social workers came to tell me about him. The words they used to describe Cory were heartbreaking: they labeled him a bully, angry, uncontrollable, and evil.

It was shocking to me that they felt it was perfectly acceptable to label any child "evil," let alone a first grader. When they said "evil," I knew immediately that it was all about pain.

I wondered how this little boy, after being in school only two years, could have warranted such criticism and disdain. So, I did one of my 30 Second TurnArounds on them and said, "Wow, he must be in so much pain." The expressions on their faces instantly transformed to one of realization, a soft *oh* mixed with a thoughtful *hmm*, as if they had never considered that perspective before.

Energy Hack #1: High Vibe It

Suspend Judgment

Over the next several months, in my support group for boys, I came to know Cory well enough to know that he was neither evil nor uncontrollable.

Then, one day, he threw a chair at his teacher. Since the principal was out of the building at the time, Cory was sent to my office. Something was off! I knew that he had never previously acted with this much violence, and now it was time to get to the heart of the matter.

Energy Hack #2: What, If, When It

Compassionate Curiosity

I sat down on a chair that put me at his eye level, and I asked him what had hurt him so much that he would throw a chair at his teacher.

He replied that his teacher hated him and always had. He felt there was no way to ever get her to like him. So, I asked him if he would tell his teacher this with my help. He agreed, and I arranged for her to come to my office. As we talked to the teacher, I supported Cory in expressing his feelings. His teacher said that she didn't hate him, and, in fact, she liked him but was afraid of him.

Then I asked Cory what had happened that he felt that she hated him, and he replied that he knew he was a very, very bad boy, and he didn't think anyone could ever like him. I was impressed by his ability to articulate his deep-seated belief about himself.

Energy Hack #3: ReLabel It

No Labels No Limits

I put one arm on his shoulders, put my other hand on his heart and started affirming what a wonderful, delightful, lovable child I saw him to be. I explained to him the truth about himself. I told him that it was not about being bad at all, just that he sometimes lashed out at other people because he hurt so much himself.

I complimented him on just how well I saw him doing in group, and how I saw him taking some risks with expressing his feelings. I affirmed that I knew he would be able to express how he was feeling even better and better as time went on. I told him that, as we worked on how to talk about what he was worried about, instead of throwing things, it would make it easier to be friends with the other kids and his teachers.

I wanted to instill in Cory new, life-affirming thoughts about himself. So I continued to reinforce what a wonderful, good, sweet boy I considered him to be. I pointed out how special and brave he was for the work he was doing with me in learning how to express his hurt feelings.

I told him how proud I was of him on the playground and in class for all the efforts I saw him making and that more and more children were liking him. I expressed my belief in his ability to ask for what he needed.

As I was speaking to him, I gradually felt the weight of his entire
body coming to rest on my right hand as he leaned into me.
His eyes were glazed over.
It was a moment in time
unlike anything I had experienced before.
Like a dry sponge, he was drinking in
my affirmation of him into his entire being.

     CHANGE YOUR VIBE, SEE YOUR KIDS THRIVE

Up to this point, his teacher had feared having him in her classroom because she believed he was an evil boy.

Cory's energetic interpretation of her labeling and her fear of him left him confused, powerless, and hurting. It's natural for children to strike back when they feel hurt because they think they are bad.

An adult must take the responsibility to help shed light on what has been causing the hurt in the child's life. Any aggressive act warrants immediate heart connecting investigation and resolution.

As I finished speaking, I gently stood him back up. Cory's teacher said she regretted not realizing his pain, then gave him a hug, told him she loved him, and took him back to class. It is my belief that the reversing of Cory's labels had everything to do with the dramatic improvement in his behavior which followed this incident into the remainder of the school year.

How long did this all take?

Maybe it took 30 seconds, perhaps it took 60 seconds to get to the heart of the problematic behavior and relabel Cory.

Let's review how I used each of my 3 Energy Hacks—*High Vibe It, What, If, When It,* and *ReLabel It*—during my short, yet life changing, process with Cory.

High Vibe It: Throughout my interactions with Cory, I focused on creating and maintaining a non-judgmental atmosphere—an AFZ: Attitude Free Zone.

From the outset, when I learned about how adults in his life had labeled him as "evil," I consciously decided to approach him with compassion and an AFZ.

Rather than reflecting the negativity surrounding his reputation, I maintained an energy of affirmation and belief in his potential. This high-vibe energy not only encouraged Cory but also created a safe space where he could begin to explore his feelings without the weight of others' judgment.

What, If, When It: The *What, If, When Method* was crucial when Cory acted out by throwing a chair. Instead of reacting with immediate reprimand or suspension, I decided to connect with him on a deeper level.

When I asked, "What hurt you so much that you threw a chair at your teacher?" I opened the door for him to get to the heart of it by reaching for his thoughts first and his feelings second.

This was essential, as it shifted the focus from his behavior to the underlying pain causing it.

When he expressed that he believed his teacher hated him, I followed up with, "If you could tell her how you feel, what would you say?" This empowered him to contemplate a constructive dialogue and build trust in our relationship.

Finally, I reassured him with, "When you're ready, let's talk to her together." This gave him a sense of ownership over his feelings and encouraged him to engage skillfully with those around him.

ReLabel It: The relabeling process was perhaps the most transformative aspect of our interactions. Cory had internalized labels like "bully" and "evil," which clearly influenced his behavior.

I took the time to affirm and reinforce his true nature by telling him repeatedly that he was a "good, wonderful, delightful, lovable" child.

By highlighting his strengths and bravery in learning to express his worries, I helped him begin to reshape his self-identity away from negativity. The moment I affirmed his worth and saw him absorb those words, it was clear that this new narrative was taking hold.

Something To Think About

My use of *High Vibe It, What, If, When It*, and *ReLabel It* not only transformed the way Cory viewed himself, but it also fostered a deeper understanding between him and his teacher, leading to a self-sustaining change in his behavior.

These energy hacks are powerful tools for transformation, reminding us that when we approach opportunities with compassionate curiosity, we can create lasting impacts in the lives of children.

But this is not all, is it?

What was his punishment?

Thank you for asking. Let's get into it.

CHAPTER 26

THE HIDDEN CURRENTS

Understanding the Impact of Adult Energy on Children

In the world of education, the responsibility of shaping young lives lies rightfully on the shoulders of adults. Yet, amid the hustle and bustle of daily interactions, many adults overlook a critical truth: their attitudes and behaviors toward children wield immense power.

When we dismiss or disparage the very students we are tasked with guiding, we not only risk damaging their self-esteem but also create an environment fraught with misunderstanding and conflict.

I invite us to pause and reflect on the importance of accountability, urging all adults to recognize that their words and actions carry weight and consequences. Just as children must learn to navigate the complexities of their emotions and relationships, so too must we, as caregivers and educators, confront the implications of our treatment of them.

By acknowledging our role in shaping perceptions and experiences, we can begin a journey of transformation—one where accountability fosters not only personal growth but a more supportive and nurturing atmosphere for the children in our care.

As we explore the dynamics of adult attitudes toward children, it is crucial to consider the consequences of those attitudes.

Punishment? Consequences?

Now I know what many will be asking, "But what was the punishment for throwing a chair at his teacher? What was the consequence?"

Here's the thing: in that miraculous moment, in that turnaround moment, you'd simply have to be there to fully feel the totality of the change that took place inside of him.

> To make this about giving him a harsh punishment
> at this very vulnerable moment would be like
> —I'm going to say it again—pushing Cory to the
> ground, putting your foot on his shoulder,
> and yelling at him to get up!

You would be taking this exquisitely beautiful transformation and completely negating it by issuing consequences after a palpable experience of this magnitude.

Now, understand that, had that incident not been the end of it, he and his teacher, parents, principal, and I would get together to determine if there would need to be a restorative consequence, such as making amends, perhaps even by both parties.

And this is the part I think a lot of people miss: we are in skill development mode. We're in collaboration mode. We would explore what skills needed to be taught. For instance, what Cory would need to learn to do or say when he was picking up on hateful vibes and feeling judged.

But we're not done yet. I have three points I want to make here, because someone must step up and make them, and it might as well be me.

Let's keep going.

The first point I want to make is that when the adults in the building speak disparagingly about children, such as calling them "evil," what is the consequence for them?

What is the consequence for the adults?

Because what we're expecting children to do is to overcome the attitudes, vibes, and tones directed toward them by the adult in the room. We're asking it, we're expecting it, and we're getting disappointed in a child if the child doesn't respond or react well when the adult in the room may not like them or may fear them.

Now, I know a lot of parents and teachers today are concerned about their own safety, which is why I want to tell you this story.

Because until you figure out what's really going on for a kid, until you get to the heart of it and find out what prompted an implosion or explosion, you are missing the main piece to the puzzle. Without this piece, you will not advance a child's life for the better.

My **second point** is that, while these adults labeled Cory as "evil" when speaking to each other, I never heard any of them convey this directly to him. Their attitudes, vibes, and tones did. How shocking is it that when I asked him what had hurt him so badly that he picked up his chair and threw it at his teacher, he answered without hesitating, "She hates me. She hates me. I'm bad. I'm so bad."

I do not believe his teacher ever said this to him directly. She was a very kind and loving teacher. I believe that, as she said, her fear of not being able to control him when he was angry was vibing at him all day every day, and to him it felt like hate.

Doesn't your heart just break? What is a kid to do? What skills do we need to teach today's children, to help them come up over the attitudes, vibes, and tones of not only their teachers, but also their peers and family members?

As with our first three experiments: Influencer-Receiver, IKEA, and Dr. Emoto, Cory absorbed and metabolized the "evil" label into his neurophysiology every single day.

What is a kid supposed to do? He was only a first grader! There was an energetic chasm that he couldn't figure out how to fill, how to be accepted, welcomed, wanted, and most importantly, valued, liked, and yes, even loved.

You will remember that, in my *Lemons to Lemonade* story, Mrs. A. was not reprimanded and never apologized to me. This is a mistake we make as adults, thinking that we don't need to apologize or atone for our tone.

Cory's teacher told her truth and took responsibility for her part, an essential part of the success story. I hope you see how powerful taking ownership is in getting to the heart of any problem.

Finally, my **third point** is the obvious fact that we have a lot of bullying and violence in our schools today. We have kids bringing guns to school and shooting their peers and their teachers. Until we address the elephant in the room, these implosive and explosive problems will not ever go away. And the elephant in the room is our attitudes, vibes, and tones.

This is a vast problem that can be remedied, but not without the willingness of the adults in these kids' lives to be accountable for what we think, say, and do to the children in our care, inadvertently or not.

Here's the great news: there's transformative power and energy in holding a reasonable and high expectation.

> Children are like sponges.
> They soak up everything you say and think.
> What you speak is what you think;
> your thoughts have energy.

You've heard the saying, "What you attend to, you bring about; where attention goes, energy flows." As you've been learning, quantum interconnectedness, the measurable evidence-based science, shows you beyond the shadow of a doubt that your connections are energetic in nature. Remember, Einstein asserted: Everything Is Energy!

Whether you mean to cause harm or not doesn't matter; of course, it's inadvertent. But you are the adult in the room. Whether you're a teacher or a parent, you have the power to influence based on what you're thinking, what you're saying, and what you're energetically infusing children with.

Something To Think About

Cory's story illustrates the power of the label to generate more of the same. So, since labeling is pervasive in our society, and I don't think I will be able to stop that, then let's relabel proactively where needed and do so affirmatively.

What we can do with life-limiting labels and diagnoses is turn them around into something affirmative and life-enhancing. That was all that Corey needed. He needed an adult who could understand the energy he was reacting to, and then intercede on his behalf with the adults in charge of his world. Just like relabeling Cory, you will see in the next chapter how I also relabeled an entire class from having been the biggest, baddest to be the biggest, best class. And it worked.

Because you are here, I suspect that you have kids you think can't be fixed and are impossible. You may feel really bad about yourself, but that's not getting it solved. That's not creating change. You want to make a difference with the power of your connection, your energetic connection, and I'm excited for you to learn how easy and fun it is to relabel yourself and others.

Find out in my Micro-Dose resource at: NoLabelsNoLimits.com

So often it feels like we're not making a significant difference, so remember this always:

> You receive the instant you give and, in that,
> you can trust you've made a difference in someone's life
> because you felt it in your own.

CHAPTER 27

CRAZY JOSH AND THE BIGGEST, BADDEST SIXTH GRADE CLASS

A Defining Year

I had just been hired at my second school, in what would be my third year of teaching. For the first time, I was teaching just one grade level—the sixth grade. But this was anything but your ordinary sixth grade! I was hired because of my reputation as a "high-functioning disciplinarian," and it was true that kids didn't get away with anything in my class.

Although the administrators may have assumed that I was a traditional disciplinarian, in fact I wasn't. I had been transitioning from authoritarian to authoritative teaching since my first year of teaching grades 3,4,5,6 in a rural school. I had achieved the results that administrators were looking for in a new way, one that they mostly didn't understand. Since results were what they were seeking, I was hired on the spot.

This particular class required someone with stamina because, as I was told during the interview, these were "the worst bunch of kids ever in the history of this school." I asked when this bad behavior had begun, and he replied, "In kindergarten!" The principal went on to refer to them as a crew of juvenile "angry misfits" that had allegedly behaved so badly that they frightened every teacher who had worked with them for the last six years.

Not only was I supposedly inheriting the worst bunch of kids, I was also getting Crazy Josh, as the teachers had privately labeled him. He was a sixth-grader with some physical disabilities and, by today's standards, would have been considered an Alphabet Soup kid. But Josh hadn't yet come face to face with my "Magic!" That was my stock in trade.

One reason why I had so much success with children, and why I was becoming a very good TurnAround Specialist, was that I had been given so many limiting labels as a kid. No matter how hard I tried, the labels stuck. My parents couldn't see me any other way than what they'd already decided about me.

So I had a certain deep empathy with all of the children. And, moreover, it made me discerning and downright determined to prove all of the other teachers wrong. I admit that I definitely had an attitude toward all the other teachers, but at that young age, I really didn't care what they thought. The prospect of proving them wrong thrilled me.

I suppose this was one way I tried to heal what my parents had unknowingly done with me, by labeling me so disparagingly. When you're convinced that you are *less than*, it's important to learn that you can choose to do it differently. That's a significant lesson for all of us, to know that we all have within us an intuitive and empathetic understanding of how to turn things around.

     CHANGE YOUR VIBE, SEE YOUR KIDS THRIVE

On the first day of school, the sixth-grade kids walked in, acting as if they were indeed the "biggest and baddest." They wanted to be sure that I knew just how bad they were! I knew all right, and I also knew that I was going to have to play this "straight, clean, and right down to the line." I was going to have to remain mentally disciplined and prevent limiting labels from entering my mind.

Whenever a teacher would tell me bad things about certain kids, or this group in particular, I would deliberately develop "selective amnesia." It became the year when I first started relabeling my students.

This class needed my *vision* for them, despite themselves.

When school began, the first thing the kids wanted to know was if I had "heard about them." Now that was an understatement! But instead of answering their question, I asked them what they thought I'd been told and, word for word, they confirmed the information I had been given by the staff. Then I gave them a pep talk to beat all pep talks. I began by telling them that I didn't believe a word I had been told, and that by Christmas, they would have forgotten all about it too. They hooted; obviously they didn't believe me. Being the biggest, baddest class this school had ever seen was their identity. It made them special, and they couldn't see any other way to distinguish themselves in any positive way.

Although they appeared proud of their reputation, I knew that it hurt their hearts terribly to be told over and over again how bad they were. I could feel it in my soul, and I could tell they wanted to find a way out. However, they didn't yet trust me to lead them to a better place and certainly could not believe in themselves or their goodness. So, I was going to have to prove myself and help them to develop self-trust.

Now, seated at a desk in the middle of the classroom was an undersized, gangly boy whose behavior was outlandish. Whenever I would walk over to talk to him, he'd turn off his hearing aid and screw up his face, in an effort to look just as crazy as he could. I smiled at him and asked him his name. He was surprised that I didn't already know it. Of course I knew it; nobody but a kid labeled "Crazy Josh" would be acting like this. But, with my decision to develop a case of "selective amnesia," I was attitudinally—energetically—clean. I acted as though he were a stranger and that I was glad to be getting acquainted with him as his new teacher.

I could tell that this surprised him and threw him off guard. He didn't know how to react to my acceptance of him, so he responded with more crazy behavior. I smiled, mentally sent him some love vibes, and continued to converse with him as if he were acting in a perfectly normal manner.

That's all I did—repeatedly. It would simply take some time and some loving kindness to move him out of the "crazy" label. Instead of being resistant to his outlandish behavior, I was inclusive, pulling him into the class and the activities. Yet whenever he became frustrated with the work, he would revert to his crazy actions.

Instead of addressing Josh's big behavior, I concentrated on his frustration with the task. That's all. Because his behavior was so noticeably disruptive, it was hard for his previous teachers to ignore. So, they labeled his behavior crazy rather go to work on the underlying causes. The result was mutual dislike and constant discord. In fact, by fifth grade, Josh's classroom tolerance had diminished to the piont where he couldn't handle the previous teacher's intolerance of him. By the end of that school year, he would implode and explode two to three times per week. He would be reprimanded and sent home or sent to a special education teacher.

　　　CHANGE YOUR VIBE, SEE YOUR KIDS THRIVE

Resistance, rejection, exclusion, and seclusion are the most hurtful—de-energizing—techniques we can use to try to curb unproductive behavior. And yet, it's so common for adults experiencing DARPing to slip into these modes of control. They will never be successful, because they aim to suppress behavior, not to deal with its causes. However, by assessing the situation and ferreting out underlying causes of the behavior, it may be possible to find a way to resolve the source. If you can do that successfully, the unacceptable behavior will be resolved.

There's no doubt that Josh was a problematic case, but I made up my mind that, before the school year was out, he would be main-streamed back into the classroom, full time and fully functional.

It took about nine long weeks of trials, tests, and tribulations, but I won the whole class over. I was determined enough to pull it off. Maybe I loved them so much because they were all so much like me at that age.

By February, Josh no longer wanted to go to Special Ed because he didn't want to miss out on what we were doing together in the classroom. He experienced what it felt like to be included as one of the kids in his class, and he began to thrive personally, academically, and show even more of his wit and humor.

Six years later, I received the graduation pictures from the small-town paper. All the kids looked great, but Josh had grown up to be quite handsome. Not only was I delighted to see that this boy was a graduate, but I admit there were tears in my eyes when I read of his scholarship to attend the nearby community college.

You Can't Have an Attitude and Keep It A Secret!

Josh was a child whose life was threatened by a powerful label and the disparaging attitudes of those around him. He was "crazy" and was among "the baddest of the bad." So, as a self-fulfilling prophecy, his behavior kept matching the label. It's no surprise his "sit down and shut up" teachers held an intolerant attitude toward him! He was on a downward spiral, unless some adult decided to step in and break the cycle, starting with relabeling him.

When we get in touch with our attitudes, beliefs, and resistances about any concerning situation we may be dealing with, we, ourselves, will be transformed. And when we are personally transformed, we set new energy in motion that will instantaneously affect the lives of those whom we touch, whether they are in the same room with us or halfway around the world. A shift in attitudinal energy is felt: your message has been sent and received!

Something To Think About

As we reflect on my year with Crazy Josh and the "biggest, baddest" sixth-grade class, let's take a moment to break down how I effectively used what became my top 3 Energy Hacks—*High Vibe It, What, If, When It,* and *ReLabel It*—to create a transformative environment for both Josh and the entire classroom. These strategies weren't just theoretical; they were practical tools that made a significant difference.

High Vibe It: From the very beginning, because of my own childhood, I understood how crucial it was to set a confident, welcoming, energetic tone in the classroom. Instead of allowing the detrimental labels and stories I had heard about the students to define my interactions with them, I took the opportunity to develop "selective amnesia." This was my way of consciously choosing to focus only on the potential I saw in the kids, regardless of their past behaviors.

   CHANGE YOUR VIBE, SEE YOUR KIDS THRIVE

By holding the intention of "Best Class Ever," I cultivated an environment where the students felt they could thrive. Remember, when we elevate our own energy, we naturally influence those around us to raise theirs, too.

What, If, When It: This method became particularly vital in working with Josh. Rather than focusing solely on his disruptive behavior, I shifted the conversation towards understanding his angst and frustrations. By asking questions like, "What's going on for you that you acted like that?" or "If you did know, what might it be?" I opened the door for Josh to explore his emotions without fear of judgment. And if he wasn't ready to reply, I reassured him with, "When you do know, let's talk." This approach helped him take ownership of his actions, fostered self-awareness, and encouraged him to trust himself, and me. It's essential to provide that safe space for our students to reflect and grow, as it lays the groundwork for transformation.

ReLabel It: Finally, I made it my mission to help Josh and his classmates, shed the harmful labels they had been given over the years. By consistently using affirmative and empowering language, I relabeled their identities to align with the potential I saw in them. Instead of calling Josh "Crazy," I highlighted his sense of humor, his creativity, and his many contributions to the class. This relabeling process allowed him to redefine who he was, moving away from the limitations of past identities. We all have the power to change the narrative. By promoting healthy self-perceptions, we enable our students to envision a brighter future for themselves.

As we summarize this experience, let's appreciate how these energy hacks offered a roadmap for profound transformational change—not just for Josh, but for the entire classroom. By fostering a high-vibe atmosphere, engaging students with the *What, If, When Method,* and relabeling their identities, I demonstrated that we can create a powerful ripple effect of positivity and growth.

Remember, these strategies are not just tools for educators but can be applied in all areas of life, and not just with children.

When we shift our energy, perspectives, and the way we perceive others, we not only change our own experiences but also set into motion a wave of empowerment for those around us.

To explore the complete story about the biggest, baddest sixth-grade class and the energy hacking that can revolutionize your impact and accelerate learning (average 2.5 to 3 years' growth), I invite you to watch my free webinar at: AcademicSuccess101.com

So, let's carry these lessons forward, embracing the potential within ourselves and those we seek to uplift!

CHAPTER 28

THE POWER OF OWNING IT

The Energetic Freedom "Owning It" Gives You

In a world that often prioritizes deflection or defensiveness over personal accountability, the simple act of acknowledging the effects of our thoughts, words, and actions stands out as a powerful practice.

Owning our missteps, oversteps, and failures to fulfill our responsibilities isn't just about taking responsibility—it's about liberating ourselves from the chains of guilt, shame, and resentment that are often self-imposed.

There is remarkable freedom in quickly stepping up, apologizing, asking for forgiveness, and atoning for our mistakes. This elevates our energetic intelligence and strengthens our resiliency.

In this chapter, we will explore the transformational power of owning our actions and participation, examining how this practice can fundamentally reshape our relationships and our self-perception. We are here to make a difference.

But first, let me share the creed I came up with as my North Star.

Difference Maker's Creed

When I make a mistake:
I will own it quickly and make necessary amends
to all those I've upset.

When I have success:
I will celebrate what's happened and shine my light
warmly to include others.

When someone is hurting:
I will lean in quietly and compassionately to ask
if I can help in any way.

When someone disrespects me:
I will be curious about "what's going on for them"
instead of making it about me.

When someone is closed-minded:
I will be receptive to other people's ideas,
perspectives, cultures, and beliefs.
—Mary Robinson Reynolds

Available for you to download as my gift to you as
a beautiful pdf to print: MaryReynolds.com/DMC

Embracing Accountability

When we find ourselves in situations where we've hurt someone—whether intentionally or unintentionally—our default patterns often drive us to respond in unproductive ways.

We might deflect blame, justify our actions, pose distracting "what about" questions, or choose silence to avoid the discomfort of confrontation. However, none of these responses lead to resolution and repair.

Instead, the hurt festers, creating an energetic chasm, not only between us and the person we've wronged, but also within ourselves.

Each unacknowledged mistake weighs heavily on our hearts, minds, and impacts our nervous system.

Our family has embraced a simple yet profoundly effective practice that our son discovered for himself, which enabled him to move on quickly from upsets without ruminating.

It empowers us all to move past upsets quickly. It's as simple as saying,

"I'm sorry. Please forgive me for all of it."

That's it.

There is no need for excuse-making or JREDDing—Justifying, Rationalizing, Explaining, Defending, or Debating.

In owning what you've done—using *What, If, When It* with yourself—you can lower your shame completely by simply getting to the heart of what was going on for you at the time you hurt someone else. (Yelled, slapped, diminished, demoralized, made fun of, or being an unfiltered, mean-spirited, brutal truth sayer.)

Ownership is a powerful, transformative vibe.

This straightforward acknowledgment serves as a soothing balm, healing emotional wounds and freeing us all from the unnecessary weight of ruminating over past mistakes.

By vocalizing our accountability and seeking forgiveness, we are able to not only heal the rift but also affirm our own humanity and capacity for growth.

The Importance of Ownership

Many individuals struggle with the notion of ownership, particularly in a culture that increasingly normalizes entitlement.

While we celebrate individuality and self-expression, the refusal to accept responsibility has become alarmingly common.

In such an environment, it's all too easy for people to harm others and then adopt a victim mentality.

This deflection perpetuates cycles of hurt and resentment, energetically weakening not just the instigator but also the victim, who finds themselves in a state of emotional distress.

As I always told our children growing up:

Do the thing that takes the courage.

What if, instead, we chose courage over entitlement?

What if we were willing to say, "I made a mistake. I hurt you, and for that, I'm truly sorry. Please forgive me."

Such statements are liberating, not just for those who hear them but also for those who speak them. In acknowledging our missteps, we strip away the layers of defensiveness that keep us isolated and exposed to our own insecurities. We get to embrace our humanity.

Here's where many adults accidentally undo their ownership:

    CHANGE YOUR VIBE, SEE YOUR KIDS THRIVE

"I'm sorry I yelled, but you won't stop bugging me!"

So, "own it" means own all of it. A statement like this teaches a child that they caused your behavior.

Or saying something like, "I was just so stressed from work, so I yelled at you because you are so needy right now."

Once again, explaining your reaction by blaming the child for it puts the burden on the child to understand and regulate your emotions.

Own all of it. Stop JREDDing. Just own what was going on for you and stop talking. Put a period on it. Seriously, just stop talking!

Here's a better example of getting to the heart of it: "It scared me so much when you ran into the street. I got angry and yelled instead of telling you how much I love you and how I want you to be safe. Please promise me that you will always look both ways before you cross the street."

Here's the beautiful part: Owning what was going on for you and apologizing for how you reacted doesn't erase what happened, but it changes how the event is stored in the child's memory.

When you explain to a child how much their actions scared you and how much you love them, you create a more memorable impact than simply yelling and threatening them for something they did impulsively.

Next time, they'll remember your love instead of the agitated energy of your fear and frustration.

By coming back to take responsibility, you're actively reshaping the emotional meaning of that moment.

The Power of Vulnerability – Dialing Off Shame

There is immense power in vulnerability.

Our society often equates strength with invincibility, assuming a facade that claims we are immune to failure or pain.

Yet, in reality, it is in our most vulnerable moments that we find our most profound strength.

When we are our most vulnerable, we are our most powerful.

By letting our defenses down, we reveal our authentic selves, allowing connections to deepen and understanding to flourish. This transparency fosters an environment where growth can occur, not only for ourselves but also for those around us.

When we embrace our imperfections, we invite others to do the same. Our willingness to acknowledge our wrongs can create a ripple effect, encouraging those in our lives to adopt a similar approach.

Imagine a community built on the foundation of acknowledgment, where everyone feels safe to express themselves without fear of judgment or retribution.

In such a space, transformation becomes possible—as we support each other through our missteps rather than blaming or hiding from them.

Finding Freedom

Ultimately, the practice of owning our part is a pathway to energetic intelligence, resiliency, and freedom.

When we confront our mistakes directly, we sever the ties that bind us to feelings of guilt, anxiety, or shame. Instead, we create a channel for personal growth and healing.

The simple act of saying "I'm sorry" can lead to profound internal energetic shifts, allowing us to reclaim our energy, focus, and peace of mind.

So, embrace the energetically transformative power of ownership.

Let's practice humility and openness, not only in our personal lives but also in the larger tapestry of our communities.

Be A Living Example of What Humanity Can Be

In doing so, we can challenge the prevailing culture of entitlement and bring forth a more compassionate, understanding, and connected world.

If we can liberate ourselves through the simple act of owning our part, we can pave the way for deeper healing—for ourselves and for one another.

Something To Think About

When all is said and done, it's unreasonable to expect respect from someone when you treat them disrespectfully in your attitudes, vibes, and tone.

Yet, all too often, those in positions of power come down hard on the very children from whom we're demanding respect, showing them no respect simply because they are children.

I would like to bring this book to a close with a final thought for those moments when it feels like nothing is working and you're uncertain about what to do next: something I came up with decades ago that helps me turn things around quickly.

Give It Away

If you want love, give it away.
If you want respect, give it away.
If you want cooperation, give it away.
If you want compassion, give it away.
If you want joy, give it away.
If you want trust, give it away.
If you want kindness, give it away.
If you want understanding, give it away.
If you want friendship, give it away.
If you want grace, give it away.
If you want hope, give it away.
If you want forgiveness, give it away.
If you want inspiration, give it away!
If you want control, give it away!
If you want peace, give it away.
It's really very simple when you think about it.

-Mary Robinson Reynolds

CHAPTER 29

MY FINAL THOUGHTS ...

Harnessing the Power of *The Energetics of Behavior*

You Made It!

Congratulations on completing *The Energetics of Behavior*! You've explored one new crucial insight after another that will transform your interactions with today's youth and your energetically infused emotional landscape.

We live in an era where the pace of life is relentless, and the demands upon us can sometimes feel overwhelming.

Yet, by embracing the concept of energetics and the implications of quantum interconnectedness, you've equipped yourself with the knowledge and tools to deal effectively with today's opportunities.

You have learned how to quickly self- and co-regulate and to create a better environment for yourself and the young people in your life.

Take a moment to reflect on what you've learned. The energy of a situation can significantly influence the responses of both children and adults during moments of emotional escalation.

The simplified advice, relevant science, and the quick and easy energy hacks you've encountered throughout this book aren't merely theoretical—they're actionable insights you can weave into your daily routine.

By recognizing when you, or those around you, are energetically triggered, you can implement the self- and co-regulation energy hacks outlined in this book, shifting the dynamic from chaos to calm.

Remember, it's not just about managing outbursts; it's about cultivating an emotionally temperate atmosphere that nurtures connection, understanding, education, and growth.

As an adult juggling multiple responsibilities when supporting youth, you may often find yourself in a constant state of stress and readiness, in an energetically triggered emotional state, bracing for the next upheaval. But now you know that you have the power to change this narrative!

Now that you understand what it takes to master your energetic responses, empower yourself and practice self- and co-regulation by doing some energy hacking.

When the energy in the room shifts, you can be the anchor that stabilizes the situation. Transmit the peace you wish to see. In doing so, you'll not only help the young people in your care learn to self-regulate but also help them build trust and safety within.

Think about your own "energetic impact" on others. Each interaction serves as an opportunity to demonstrate the principles you've learned. Whether at home, in the classroom, or at work, you hold the power to influence how others respond in emotionally charged situations.

Start small. Experiment with your insights in day-to-day scenarios. Notice the transformations that follow. Every conscious step you take, every moment of awareness you cultivate, contributes to a larger shift.

Now that you know what you need to do, it's time to dive deeper!

As you continue working with *The Energetics of Behavior*, I want to help you move through this exciting terrain with ease and grace. That's why I've created three dynamic pathways for you to continue to explore and learn:

1. **Micro-Dose:** A collection of engaging short training videos, 20 - 90 minutes each, designed especially for busy individuals like you. These bite-sized lessons focus on helping you love, live, and work with today's youth without ever missing a beat again. Absorb these insights at your own pace, implement them swiftly, and start witnessing productive changes faster than you can believe, more often than not.

2. **Macro-Dose:** Online Courses, 2-5 hours each. Now that you understand how the energetics of behavior is coming into play, instead of swiping through Instagram for tools and tips that are all over the map, why not get a field-tested roadmap that will get you where you need to be going with today's children with my *MAPit* and *Victim No More* Online Courses.

3. **Mastery:** Online Courses, 6+ hours, such as my *Unlocking the Energetics of Behavior: A Quantum Approach to Ending Explosive and Implosive Behaviors*. For those eager to dive deeper, this immersive course is where we roll up our sleeves and master the concept of energetics.

Don't worry; you don't need any advanced degrees to become a master at influencing energetic results. The *Unlocking the Energetics of Behavior* masterclass is crafted for all personality and learning styles and tailored for people who, like me, have too much to do and need it to be straightforward, immediately impactful, and even some FUN!

Learn the best methods for using your energetic influence to create long term change with an accumulation of short-term successes.

Less Effort, Better Results

Here's the exciting part: You will begin to see improvements in your interactions without feeling overwhelmed—there are no fire hoses of information here! Everything I've created is tailored specifically for you, the busy, proactive individual seeking the most efficient route to better results.

So, what are you waiting for?

Your path to mastery starts now. Let's make this quantum leap into the realm of energetic engagement together.

The next steps are yours to take—embrace the journey and watch as your relationships with today's youth transform for the better.

MaryReynolds.com/Programs

ABOUT THE AUTHOR

In a world where today's youth often face overwhelming influences, *The Energetics of Behavior: Change Your Vibes, See Your Kids Thrive!* emerges as not just a book, but a beacon of hope and a practical guide to healing today's children and ourselves.

I wrote this book with you in mind—busy adults who pour their hearts into nurturing the youth around them. With your full plates and endless responsibilities, I want to simplify your efforts as you manage your time and priorities.

Using my Micro-Dose gift resources woven throughout this book, I aimed to help you incorporate the concept of energetics to transform problematic behaviors into opportunities and unlock the potential within every child.

Why trust me to guide you on this journey?

I'm not just a credentialed educator. I'm a former problem child turned *Behavioral TurnAround Specialist*, with over forty years in various educational roles—including K-8 teacher, K-12 counselor, winning volleyball and basketball coach, drug, alcohol, and family counselor.

These experiences, combined with a master's degree in educational psychology, counseling, and development, have afforded me the opportunity to experience firsthand the struggles and triumphs of helping both youth and adults.

I have worked in a diverse array of environments—from rural, transient, suburban, urban schools to inner-city programs—always focused on empowering those children who have fallen through the cracks and uplifting overwhelmed parents, teachers, principals, counselors, school psychologists, and staff in problematic situations.

This wealth of experience positions me uniquely to help you quickly self- and co-regulate, allowing you to meet the needs of today's children with confidence.

Now is the moment for transformation!

The Energetics of Behavior has helped tens of thousands of teachers, parents, and educational leaders overcome the ineffective, energy draining practices that have persisted over the last four decades.

Imagine watching the children in your life flourish as you learn the best ways to utilize energetics in real-world, real-time situations you face day to day.

It's time to unlock the doors to understanding and compassion.

So grab a cup of coffee, find a comfy spot, and immerse yourself in the empowering insights waiting for you with my innovative resources to change not only your own vibes but also the dynamics within your family, classroom, and community.

Together, let's make a difference in the next generation!

Come join me: MaryReynolds.com